MACROECONOMICS
Basic concepts, questions and answers

Elijah M. James, Ph.D.

Concordia University and
Dawson College, Montreal, Canada

Butterworths
Toronto

Illustrations by Samuel Daniel

CANADA:	BUTTERWORTH & CO. (CANADA) LTD. TORONTO: 2265 Midland Avenue, Scarborough, M1P 4S1
UNITED KINGDOM:	BUTTERWORTH & CO. (PUBLISHERS) LTD. LONDON: 88 Kingsway, WC2B 6AB
AUSTRALIA:	BUTTERWORTH PTY. LTD. SYDNEY: 586 Pacific Highway, Chatswood, NSW 2067 MELBOURNE: 343 Little Collins Street, 3000 BRISBANE: 240 Queen Street, 4000
NEW ZEALAND:	BUTTERWORTHS OF NEW ZEALAND LTD. WELLINGTON: 77-85 Custom House Quay, 1
SOUTH AFRICA:	BUTTERWORTH & CO. (SOUTH AFRICA) (PTY.) LTD. DURBAN: 152/154 Gale Street

Canadian Cataloguing in Publication Data

James, Elijah M.
  Macroeconomics

ISBN 0-409-84031-9

1. Macroeconomics. I. Title.

HB171.5.J26   339   C79-094160-0

For Andrea

PREFACE

The main purpose of this book is to provide the beginning student with the basic tools of macroeconomic theory. In an attempt to keep the book short, the author was forced to be selective. However, the major areas of the subject are covered, with the exception of long-term economic growth. The book should prove useful to students taking introductory macroeconomics at the college and university levels. If used in conjunction with its companion volume, *Microeconomics: Basic Concepts, Questions and Answers*, the book should be invaluable also to students preparing for their "Advanced" level and professional examinations in economics.

Dissatisfaction with the essay as a method of testing has led to the widespread use of objective testing. Economics is particularly adaptable to objective testing and the method has much to commend it. The author fears, however, that the pendulum has swung too far. Preoccupation with objective testing and the utter neglect of the essay as a testing technique has resulted in a real loss to the student. The merits of the essay form of testing are numerous. The student is given a chance to demonstrate his command of economic language and his understanding of various theories. He is given the opportunity to demonstrate creativity, and he develops the art of selecting and organizing material to produce a satisfactory answer to a question. These and other advantages will be lost in cases where the essay form is abandoned. The author contends that the best method of testing is a combination of essays and objective testing. Essays should be supplemented, not replaced, by objective testing.

Many students experience a great deal of trouble in preparing answers to essay questions. The appendix is intended to help such students. It serves a dual teaching purpose: it teaches students how to tackle essay questions, and at the same time, it increases their understanding of economic theory. Sometimes, the answer to a question goes into detail not presented in the text. The answers provided illustrate how bits of information can be assembled into a short essay to provide an answer to a given question. In this respect, particular attention should be paid to style and content.

Many key economic terms have been collected in a glossary at the end of the book. This should serve as a quick and convenient reference. Economics can be very interesting and intellectually stimulating. It is hoped that you will find the study of economics a rewarding experience.

I owe a great debt to my colleagues at Dawson College who provided a pleasant environment for the writing of this book. I am also grateful to Mrs. N. Abbas, Mr. M. Hussain, Mr. V. Kovalski, and Mr. I. Mirza for helpful comments and suggestions. My students at Dawson College and at Concordia University deserve special thanks. They have "sampled" the product at various stages and have insisted (mainly by their questions) that certain passages be clarified. I also owe a debt of gratitude to my teachers at Memorial University of Newfoundland and at the University of Toronto. Special mention must be made of my friend and colleague, Professor S. A. Alvi of Concordia University, who taught me, perhaps unknowingly, a great deal about economics.

Those who have contributed in any way to the preparation of this book deserve any credits it may receive, but I alone am responsible for any shortcomings.

Elijah M. James
Dawson College,
Montreal,
Quebec.
January 1979.

TABLE OF CONTENTS

CHAPTER 1
INTRODUCTION

WHAT IS ECONOMICS?

There is no shortage of definitions of economics. However, in this introductory study, we will not bother our heads with a catalogue of definitions. We shall, instead, offer only one simple definition of economics: *Economics is the science which studies the way in which man uses scarce resources to satisfy his wants.* In this definition, we have used the term "scarce resources". Let us investigate this term further.

THE ECONOMIST'S CONCEPT OF SCARCITY

Ordinarily, we tend to equate scarcity with smallness of quantity. The economist's concept of scarcity is somewhat different. The following example will illustrate the difference between smallness of quantity and scarcity in the economic sense. Let us consider two situations, *A* and *B*. In situation *A*, a farmer requires 200 gallons of water per day for irrigation purposes. Without any effort whatsoever, he can obtain 500 gallons of water per day. Since his requirements fall short of the amount available to him, we say that water is abundant to this farmer. Now, in situation *B*, the farmer's requirement has grown to 800 gallons of water per day, and the amount available to him has grown to 700 gallons per day. In this situation, the farmer's requirement exceeds the amount available, and we say that water is scarce to this farmer. The following table shows the two situations.

Situation	Requirement	Availability	Economic Condition
A	200 gallons	500 gallons	Abundance
B	800 gallons	700 gallons	Scarcity

Note that in situation *B*, the farmer actually has a greater quantity of water than in situation *A*, yet, in an economic sense, water is scarce in situation *B* and abundant in situation *A*. This example illustrates

1

that scarcity, in economics, refers *not* to smallness of quantity, but to a situation where the amount available falls short of the amount required.

Let us now take a look at the term "resources". These are the things that are used to make the goods and services that we use to satisfy our wants. Economists refer to them as "factors of production".

FACTORS OF PRODUCTION

Traditionally, the factors of production have been grouped into three categories: land, labour, and capital. Land refers to the source of raw materials and includes the rocks, lakes, rivers, deposits in the earth, and even the climates of various regions. Labour refers to the physical and mental powers and skills of human beings; and capital refers to man-made means of production such as machinery, plant, and equipment.

SOME BASIC DEFINITIONS

Commodities. The term commodities is used to cover two terms — goods and services. A *good* is anything that is tangible and which satisfies our wants. Examples of goods are bread, milk, apples, clothes and refrigerators. *Services* are intangible and include transportation services, medical services, laundry services, etc. Goods can be further classified as durable consumer goods, non-durable consumer goods, and capital goods or producer goods.

Durable consumer goods or simply *consumer durables* provide services over a long period of time. Examples of durable consumer goods are a suit of clothes, a pair of shoes, a refrigerator, motor cars, washing machines.

Non-durable consumer goods provide satisfaction directly and last for a short period of time. They are consumed once they are used, whereas consumer durables are used a repeated number of times. Examples of non-durable consumer goods are bread, icecream, cigarettes, whiskey.

Capital goods or *producer goods* have already been defined above as one of the factors of production. They are not usually bought by consumers. They are bought by producers to be used to manufacture consumer goods and services.

Production. Production refers to the act of making goods and services. The act of making cars on an assembly line or of making bread in a bakery is easily seen as an act of production. But the dentist, the lawyer, and the school teacher are also engaged in production. They produce services.

Consumption.   Consumption is the act of using commodities. When you drink a glass of wine, you engage in an activity called consumption, and when you use a typewriter to type a letter or a term paper, you also engage in an act of consumption. In one case, you consume the good directly. In the other case, you consume the services provided by the good.

THE ECONOMIC PROBLEM

A little reflection will reveal that we do not have enough resources to produce all the goods and services that we need to satisfy our wants. Moreover, our wants seem to be unlimited. New wants are continually being created. This means that we are faced with the ever present problem of choice. We have to decide which wants will be satisfied and which ones will go unsatisfied. We are faced with the economic problem of how to make the best use of our scarce resources.

Since we cannot produce all the goods and services we need to satisfy our wants, it follows that every decision to produce one good involves a decision not to produce some other good. If we choose to produce good *A* instead of good *B*, then the *opportunity cost* of *A* is *B*. If a carpenter has material which he can use to produce either a table or three chairs, and if he decides to produce the table, then the opportunity cost of the table is the three chairs that could have been produced instead.

The concepts of scarcity, choice and opportunity cost can be well illustrated by the *production possibility curve*. Assume that an economy can produce only two classes of goods, *X* and *Y*. The production possibilities of this economy may be represented by the following table.

Possibilities	Quantity of X	Quantity of Y
A	0	20
B	1	16
C	2	12
D	3	8
E	4	4
F	5	0

If the economy puts all its resources into the production of Y, it could produce 20 units of Y and none of X (possibility A). The economy could put all its resources into the production of X and obtain 5 units of X but none of Y. This is possibility F. Possibilities A and F are extreme cases. Between these extreme cases, there are other possibilities. For example, the economy could choose possibility B. By giving up (sacrificing) 4 units of Y (i.e., by producing 16 units of Y instead of 20), the economy could obtain 1 unit of X. The opportunity cost of 1 unit of X is 4 units of Y. Note that in this example, the same quantity of Y has to be given up each time in order to obtain an additional unit of X. That is, the example illustrates constant opportunity cost.

FIG. 1-1

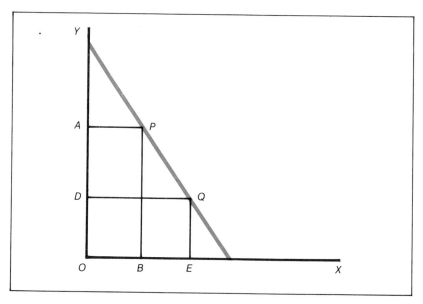

The production possibilities of the economy may also be represented by a graph called the *production possibility curve*. This is shown in Figure 1-1. Assume that the economy is operating at point P, producing OA units of Y and OB units of X. If the economy wants to increase its production of X by BE units, then it has to sacrifice AD units of Y. The opportunity cost of BE units of X is AD units of Y. Any point on the production possibility curve represents the maximum possible combination of X and Y that the economy could produce if it uses all its resources. The production possibility curve is linear (a straight line) because we assume, as we did in the case of the schedule (table) above, that the opportunity cost of an additional unit of X (or Y) is constant. This may not be the case in reality. Factors of production are not equally productive in all uses. Some resources will be more productive in the X industry than in the Y industry, and some will be more productive in the Y industry than in the X industry. As resources are shifted from industry X to industry Y, the cost is likely to increase since these resources are likely to be less productive in industry Y.

The situation of increasing cost is illustrated in the following table.

Possibilities	Quantity of X	Quantity of Y
A	0	22
B	1	18
C	2	13
D	3	7
E	4	0

The table illustrates that in order to obtain the first unit of X, the economy must sacrifice 4 units of Y. The second unit of X costs 5 units of Y. This is therefore a case of increasing opportunity cost.

If we were to plot these figures on a graph, we would obtain a production possibility curve which is concave to the origin as shown in Figure 1-2. A concave production possibility curve therefore represents increasing opportunity cost.

FIG. 1-2

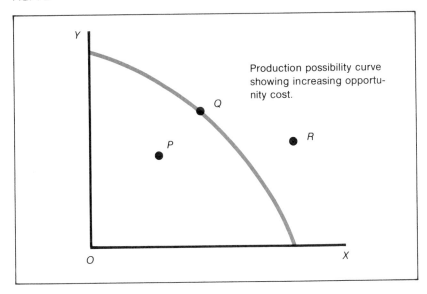

Production possibility curve showing increasing opportunity cost.

If the economy is operating with full employment of all resources, then it would be at a point on the curve, such as Q. It is unlikely that all resources will be fully employed at any particular time, hence we are likely to find the economy operating at a point below its production possibility curve. A point such as P represents unemployment of resources. The economy does not have enough resources to enable it to produce a combination represented by R. This combination is therefore unattainable. If more resources become available, or if the productivity of the existing factors increases, then the economy will be able to produce more goods and services, that is, there will be economic growth. Economic growth is represented by an outward shift of the production possibility curve as shown in Figure 1-3.

FIG. 1-3

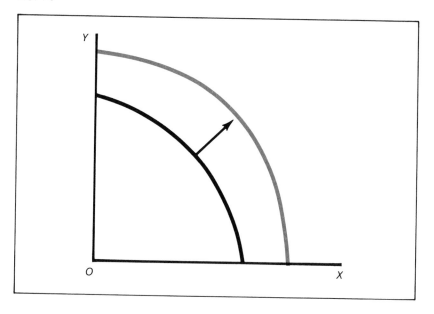

CHAPTER 2
THE ECONOMIC SYSTEM

THE ECONOMIC SYSTEM

There are many types of economic systems. The type of economic system with which we will be concerned is a mixed economy. A mixed economy is a mixture of free enterprise and government intervention. In this type of economic system, private individuals are allowed to own factors of production, prices and incomes are determined by market forces (i.e., by demand and supply), but the system is regulated by the government. The government also plays an important role in the allocation of resources. The economic system consists of economic agents who engage in economic activity. Economic activity involves production, consumption and exchange of goods and services.

ECONOMIC AGENTS

Economic agents are those individuals who take part in economic activities. This, of course, includes everybody. For purposes of economic analysis, we classify economic agents into three groups: consumers, producers, and government authorities. We also refer to these groups as the decision-making units. The term consumer refers to the household. It is the consuming unit and therefore has to make decisions regarding consumption. Since the household also owns factors of production, it has to make decisions regarding the sale of those factors of production. The producer or firm is the producing unit. It has to decide how to combine the factors of production to produce commodities. The term government authorities refers to all levels of government. They enter the market both as consumers and as producers.

THE OBJECTIVES OF THE DECISION-MAKERS

In economics, we assume that the household tries to maximize its satisfaction; that the firm tries to maximize its profits, and that the government's objectives coincide with the national economic objec-

tives. The following seem to be among the economic objectives of most nations:
a high level of employment;
relative price stability;
promotion of economic growth;
reduction of income inequality;
a favourable balance of trade.
The following table summarizes the decision-making units and their objectives.

Decision-making unit	Objective
Consumer or household	Utility (satisfaction) maximization.
Producer or firm	Profit maximization
Government	Objectives consistent with the national objectives of full employment, price stability, etc.

PRICES IN OUR ECONOMIC SYSTEM

Prices play a central role in our economic system. We may define prices as value expressed in terms of money. We shall see that our economic system functions largely through a system of prices and markets which has been referred to as the *price system* or the *market mechanism*. For the moment, let us see how the economic activities of consumers and producers are governed by the system of prices and markets. Let us consider first the economic problem of what to produce. Consumers indicate, indirectly, to producers what to produce. They do so by their actions in the market. By buying good *A* rather than good *B*, consumers are indicating to producers that good *A* rather than good *B* should be produced. Of course, other things being equal, good *A* will have a higher price than good *B*, and would therefore be more profitable to the producer. Because it is the consumer who decides what is actually produced, we refer to this phenomenon as "consumer sovereignty".

The producer has to buy the factors of production whose prices are also determined by demand and supply (i.e., by the market mechanism). Since the producer tries to produce at the lowest possible cost, he will buy more of the factors with the lowest prices and fewer of the more expensive factors. In this way, the price system determines how the factors of production are combined to produce goods and services.

Our incomes, and therefore our ability to buy goods and services, are also determined by the price system. We derive income from ownership of the factors of production. The income from labour is called wages; the income from land is called rent, and the income from capital is called interest. In a free enterprise system, all these prices of the factors of production are determined by the market. Since these prices accrue to individuals as incomes, it follows that the price system determines the size of our incomes and hence our ability to buy the goods and services produced by the economy.

To conclude, we may note that the price system determines what goods and services are produced, how those goods and services are produced, and who is able to buy those goods and services. These decisions are at the very heart of the problem of scarcity and choice. They constitute *the economic problem* (i.e., the problem of scarcity), hence we can say that in a free enterprise market economy, the economic problem is dealt with by a system of prices and markets. In later chapters, we shall see how economic decisions are guided by the market mechanism.

CHAPTER 3
DEMAND AND SUPPLY

The terms *demand* and *supply* feature significantly in the study of economics, but economics is much more than demand and supply. A sound knowledge of demand and supply is essential for an understanding of the workings of a market economy.

THE MEANING OF DEMAND

The demand for a commodity is not just a desire or a need for that commodity. Needs and desires must be backed up by an ability to buy. If this ability to buy is lacking, the desires, no matter how strong they may be, will not be made known in the market. When economists use the term demand, they refer to the amount of a good or service that consumers are willing to buy at a particular time. Not only must they be willing to buy, but they must also be able to buy, otherwise their desires will have no influence in the market.

THE DETERMINANTS OF DEMAND

What are the factors that will determine the amount of a commodity that people will buy? The following factors seem to be important in determining the amount of a commodity that people will buy: the price of the commodity, the incomes of the consumers, the prices of other commodities, and the tastes of the consumers. Let us consider each of these factors in turn.

The price of the commodity. The quantity of any commodity that people will buy depends on the price of that commodity. The higher the price of the commodity, the less the quantity people will be willing to buy. We will return to this relationship between quantity demanded and price a little later.

Consumers' incomes. Obviously, people's ability to purchase goods and services depends on the level of their incomes. The larger their incomes, the more goods and services they will be able to buy, and the smaller their incomes, the less will be their ability to buy goods and services.

Prices of other commodities. To discuss the influence of the prices of other commodities on the quantity of a commodity that consumers will be willing to buy, we need to define two new concepts—a complement and a substitute.

A *complement* is a good that is used in conjunction with another good. Examples of complements are motor cars and tires, coffee and cream, record players and records.

A *substitute* is a good that is used in place of another good. Examples of substitutes are coffee and tea, apples and bananas, butter and margarine.

If the price of record-players falls, the quantity of record-players that people will be willing to buy will increase. This means also that people will be willing to buy more records. Thus, if two commodities are complements, a fall in the price of one will lead to an increase in demand for the other. Also, an increase in the price of one will lead to a decrease in demand for the other.

On the other hand, if the price of coffee rises, some people will switch from coffee to tea. This means that the demand for tea will increase. Also, if the price of coffee falls, people will tend to switch from tea to coffee which is now relatively cheaper. Hence, if two commodities are substitutes, a rise in the price of one will lead to an increase in demand for the other. Also, a fall in the price of one will lead to a reduction in demand for the other.

Consumers' tastes. Naturally, the stronger the preference for a certain commodity, the more of that commodity will be bought. If people have a stronger preference for oranges than for plums, then they will tend to buy more oranges than plums. The stronger the taste for a commodity, the greater will be the demand for that commodity.

THE DEMAND SCHEDULE

We now return to the relationship established between the price of a commodity and the quantity that people will be willing to buy. We noted that the higher the price, the less will be bought, and the lower the price, the greater will be the quantity demanded. This relationship between price and quantity demanded is illustrated in the following table which is called a *demand schedule*.

Demand Schedule for Shirts

Price per shirt ($)	Quantity demanded per year (million)
$14	2
12	3
10	4
8	5
6	6
4	7
2	8

The above schedule should be read as follows: if the price of a shirt were $14, consumers would be willing to buy 2 million shirts per year. If the price were $12, they would be willing to buy 3 million, and so on.

THE DEMAND CURVE

If we draw a graph with price (P) on the vertical axis and quantity (Q) on the horizontal axis, and if we plot the various price-quantity combinations on the graph and connect them, the resulting figure would represent a demand curve. We may therefore define a demand curve as a graph which shows the various quantities of a commodity that consumers would be willing to buy at various possible prices. Figure 3-1 represents a demand curve.

THE LAW OF DOWNWARD-SLOPING DEMAND

You will notice that the demand curve slopes downward from left to right. Another way of expressing this idea is to say that there is an inverse relationship between quantity demanded and price. This inverse relationship is referred to as the law of downward-sloping demand. Why does the demand curve slope downward from left to right? There are two reasons. First, if the price of a commodity goes up, that commodity has become relatively more expensive. People will therefore substitute cheaper goods for the good whose price has risen. This is referred to as the *substitution effect*. For example, if the price of apples goes up, people will switch from apples to other fruits (bananas for example). Secondly, when the price of a commodity rises, the consumer is worse off because he gets less of the commodity for the same money outlay. In economic jargon, his real income falls. Because the consumer has suffered a loss of income, he buys less. This is referred to as the *income effect*.

FIG. 3-1

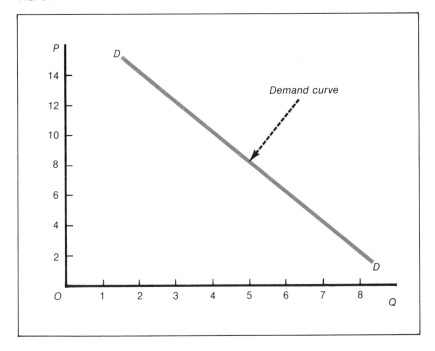

A SHIFT OF THE DEMAND CURVE vs A MOVEMENT ALONG THE CURVE

It is important not to confuse a change in demand with a change in quantity demanded. Demand refers to the whole demand curve. Hence a change in demand is represented by a shift of the entire curve. If demand increases, the entire demand curve shifts to the right as shown in Figure 3-2. It means that at *any given price*, a greater quantity will be purchased.

A decrease in demand will be represented by a leftward shift in the demand curve.

A change in quantity demanded refers to the change in quantity bought *as price changes*. In Figure 3-3, at price p_1 the quantity demanded is Q_1. As the price falls to p_2 the quantity demanded changes from Q_1 to Q_2. This is represented by a *movement along the same demand curve* from A to B.

A change in demand is brought about by a change in some factor other than the price of the commodity in question. For example, other things being equal, an increase in income will cause the demand curve to shift outward in a north-easterly direction. Other things being equal, a decrease in income will cause the demand curve to shift to the left.

FIG. 3-2

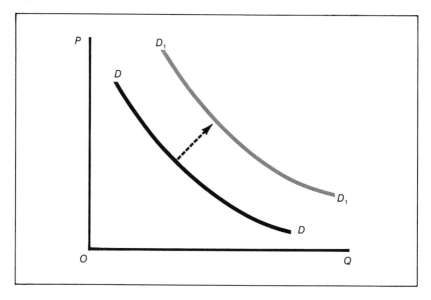

FIG. 3-3

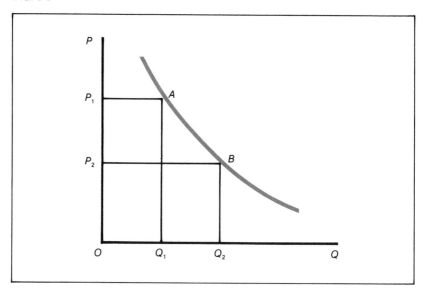

THE MEANING OF SUPPLY

Supply refers to the amount of a good or service that sellers are
willing to sell at a particular time. The term refers not to the quantities
actually sold but only to the amounts that the firms wish to sell.

THE DETERMINANTS OF SUPPLY

Among the factors influencing the quantity of a commodity that firms would be willing to sell are technology, price, and factor costs. We will consider each of these in turn.

The state of technology. Other things being equal, the higher the level of technology existing at any particular time, the greater will be the quantity produced. For example, the rapid increase in technology in the electronics field has led to a great increase in the quantity of electronic calculators produced.

The price of the commodity. The higher the price of a commodity, other things being equal, the greater will be the incentive to produce that commodity. Hence, the higher the price, the greater will be the quantity that firms would wish to offer for sale. Additional sellers may also be induced to enter the field. If the price of wheat increases, many farmers will be inclined to reduce their production of corn and increase their production of wheat.

The cost of productive factors. The firm has to purchase factors of production to manufacture commodities. Payment for these factors represents a cost to the firms. Other things being equal, the higher the cost of these factors, the less will be the quantity that a firm will be able to supply.

THE SUPPLY SCHEDULE

If we assume that all other determinants of supply except price remain constant, we will be able to study the relationship between the quantity that firms will be willing to offer for sale and the price of the commodity. We noted that the higher the price, the greater the quantity that firms will wish to sell. This direct relationship is called a *supply schedule*. A supply schedule for shirts is shown in the following table.

THE SUPPLY CURVE

If we plot these points as we did in the case of the demand curve, we will obtain a graph called the supply curve. Figure 3-4 represents a supply curve.

Supply Schedule for Shirts

Price per shirt ($)	Quantity supplied per year (million)
$2	2
4	3
6	4
8	5
10	6
12	7
14	8

The supply curve may be defined as a graph which shows the various quantities of a commodity that firms would be willing to sell at various possible prices.

FIG. 3-4

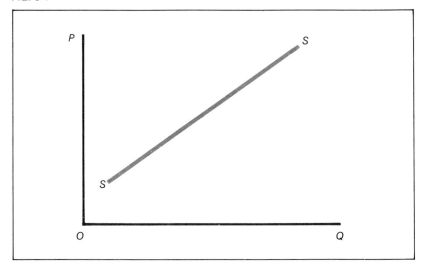

A CHANGE IN SUPPLY vs A CHANGE IN QUANTITY SUPPLIED

The distinction made between a change in demand and a change in quantity demanded applies also in the case of supply. A change in supply is represented by a *shift* of the entire supply curve while a change in quantity supplied refers to a *movement along the supply curve.* An increase in supply means that at any *given price*, firms are willing to supply a larger quantity. Figure 3-5A below represents a decrease in supply while Figure 3-5B represents a decrease in quantity supplied.

FIG. 3-5A, 3-5B

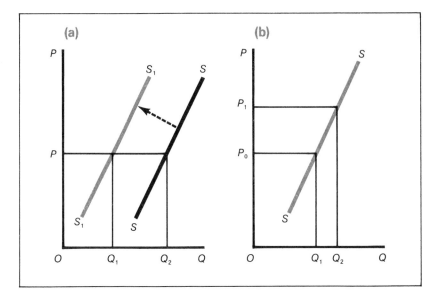

We will use the concepts developed in this chapter to see how market forces work to determine the price of a commodity.

CHAPTER 4
PRICE DETERMINATION

BRINGING DEMAND AND SUPPLY TOGETHER

In this chapter, we shall explain how the price of a commodity is determined by demand and supply. We can collect the information contained in the demand and supply schedules in the previous chapter in the following table.

Price per shirt ($)	Quantity demanded (million)	Quantity supplied (million)
14	2	8
12	3	7
10	4	6
8	5	5
6	6	4
4	7	3
2	8	2

You will notice that there is only one price at which the quantity which buyers want to buy is the same as the quantity which firms are willing to sell. This price ($8 in our example) is called the *equilibrium* price, and the quantity (5 million shirts) is called the equilibrium quantity.

The equilibrium price and quantity can also be shown on a graph. If we put the demand curve and the supply curve together on the same graph, they will intersect as shown on Figure 4-1. The intersection of the demand and supply curves gives us the equilibrium position. In the following figure, the equilibrium price is $\bar{p}$ and the equilibrium quantity is $\bar{q}$.

PREDICTIONS OF THE MODEL OF PRICE DETERMINATION

Recall that if a variable other than the price of the commodity changes, then the demand curve or the supply curve will shift. Let us examine shifts in these curves to see how the price of the commodity will be affected. This type of analysis is referred to as *comparative statics*. It involves comparing one equilibrium position with another after one variable has changed.

FIG. 4-1

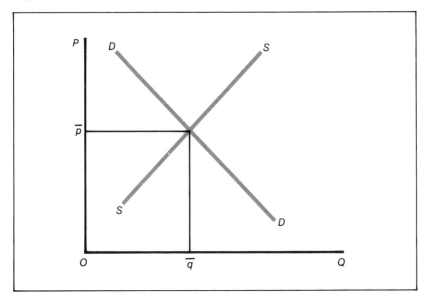

FIG. 4-2

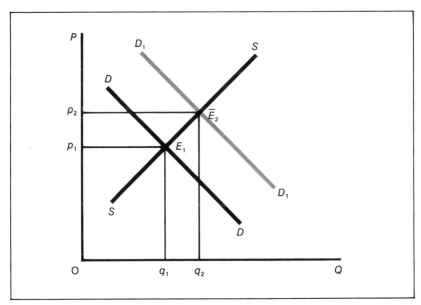

CASE 1. *An increase in demand.*

Let the demand and supply for a commodity be as shown in Figure 4-2. The equilibrium price is p_1 and the equilibrium quantity is q_1. Now let us suppose that consumers' incomes increase. Other things being equal, there will be an increase in demand for the commodity. The demand curve will shift to the right as shown in the diagram by a shift from DD to D_1D_1. The equilibrium position is now at E_2 instead of E_1. The new price is p_2 and the new equilibrium quantity is q_2. What we have demonstrated is the following proposition: *An increase in demand, other things being equal, will cause a rise in the equilibrium price and quantity.*

FIG. 4-3

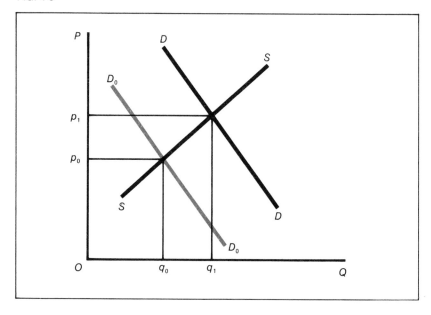

CASE 2. *A fall in demand.*

In Figure 4-3, we show that if demand falls, the demand curve shifts to the left from DD to D_0D_0. This reduction in demand may be caused by a change in taste, for example. The original equilibrium price and quantity were p_1 and q_1 respectively. The new equilibrium position is at a price of p_0 and a quantity of q_0. We have demonstrated that: *Other things being equal, a fall in demand will cause the price and quantity to fall.*

CASE 3. *An increase in supply.*

If supply increases, the supply curve shifts to the right as shown in Figure 4-4. The new equilibrium price p_0 is lower than the original price, but the equilibrium quantity has increased from q_1 to q_0. We have thus derived the following proposition: *An increase in supply, other things being equal, will cause the equilibrium price to fall and the equilibrium quantity to increase.*

FIG. 4-4

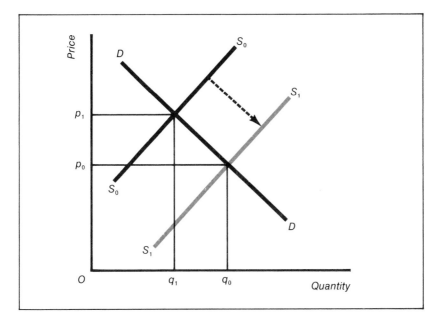

FIG. 4-5

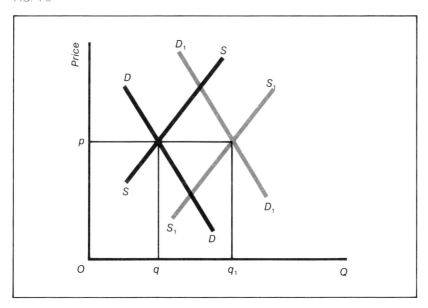

CASE 4. *A fall in supply.*

Case 4 is left as an exercise for the reader.

What can you say about the equilibrium price and quantity under the following conditions?

(a) demand increases and supply falls
(b) demand falls and supply increases
(c) demand and supply both fall
(d) demand and supply both increase.

You have probably noticed that if demand and supply move in the same direction (e.g., if both increase), we cannot say what will happen to price. It may increase, decrease, or remain unchanged depending on whether the change in demand or the change in supply is stronger. Figure 4-5 shows an increase in both demand and supply which leaves the equilibrium price unchanged. The effect on price of an increase in demand from DD to D_1D_1 is completely offset by the increase in supply from SS to S_1S_1. The equilibrium quantity, however, has increased from q to q_1.

CHAPTER 5

NATIONAL INCOME ACCOUNTING

In this chapter, we shall look at some broad economic aggregates such as gross national product, national income, total investment and total consumption. The study of the behaviour of these aggregates is the subject matter of macroeconomics. National income accounting deals with the measurement of national output and related concepts.

THE CIRCULAR FLOW OF INCOME

The flow of income in the economy is a fundamental concept in macroeconomics. The circular flow model will help us to derive certain relationships in the macroeconomy. We make the following assumptions.

1. There are only two decision-making units—consumers (households) and producers (firms).
2. Transactions between these two groups are carried on with the use of money.
3. The households own the factors of production.
4. Households and firms spend their entire income.

Figure 5-1 will help to explain the flow of income between the two groups.

The outer flow of the top loop represents the flow of factors of production from households to firms. The households receive payment for these factors of production. This payment constitutes the income of the households and is represented by the inner flow of the top loop. The firms transform the factors of production into goods and services which are sold to the households. This flow of goods and services is represented by the outer flow of the bottom loop. The payment for the goods and services is the firms' revenue. This is represented by the inner flow of the bottom loop.

The top loop represents the *factor market* since it shows the sale of factors of production by households to firms. The bottom loop represents the *product market* since it shows the sale of the firms' output (product) to the households.

Under the assumptions of the model, incomes received by the households as payment for the factors of production are passed on to the firms as payment for goods and services. The firms pass this

FIG. 5-1

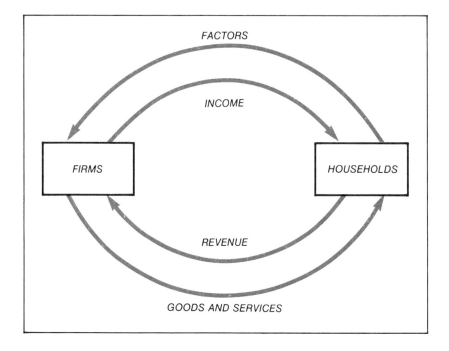

amount back to the households as payment for productive factors and so the cycle continues. This circular flow of income is in equilibrium because there is no tendency for it to increase or decrease.

INJECTIONS AND WITHDRAWALS

Let us now change the assumption that households and firms spend their entire income. Households may decide not to spend all the income they receive from the firms to purchase the output of goods and services produced by the firms. Similarly, the firms may decide not to use all their revenues received from the sale of their output to purchase factors of production from the households. In each case, the income withheld is taken out of the circular flow and is called a *withdrawal*. We will use W to denote a withdrawal. The effect of a withdrawal is to lower the level of income in the circular flow.

The firms may decide to spend more on factor services than they receive from households for their output of goods and services. The income added to the circular flow in this case is called an *injection*. We will use J to denote an injection into the circular flow. The effect of an injection is to raise the level of income in the circular flow.

In reality, injections and withdrawals occur concurrently. We know that an injection will increase the circular flow while a withdrawal will decrease it. If injections and withdrawals are happening at the same time, the effect on the circular flow would depend on the relative magnitude of the injection and the withdrawal.

If $J > W$, the circular flow will rise.

If $J = W$, the circular flow will remain constant.

If $J < W$, the circular flow will decrease.

When the injection is exactly equal to the withdrawal, the two forces are in balance and the circular flow does not change. When this happens, the circular flow is said to be in equilibrium.

GROSS NATIONAL PRODUCT (GNP)

The Gross National Product (GNP) is defined as the market value of all final goods and services produced in the economy for a given period of time (usually one year). There are two main ways of measuring GNP. These are (1) the input-factor-income approach and (2) the output-expenditure approach.

The input-factor-income approach. Measuring GNP by the factor-income approach is equivalent to evaluating the inner flow of the top loop of the circular flow in Figure 5-1. Recall that this flow is the payment for the factors of production and represents total income. But this amount is exactly equal to the output of goods and services produced by the firms. The value received by using this method is termed national income (NI).

The output-expenditure approach. It follows that we could arrive at the same value by measuring the inner flow of the bottom loop of the circular flow diagram. If we were to measure GNP by this method, we would be evaluating the expenditure on the goods and services produced, hence the name "output-expenditure" for this approach.

Problems in measurement. A number of problems arise when measuring the GNP of a country. First, we have to ensure that nothing is counted more than once, or we will be guilty of *double-counting*. Suppose there are two firms, S and C. Firm S produces steel and firm C produces chairs. Firm C buys steel from firm S to be used in the manufacture of chairs. The output of each firm is as in the following table.

If we added the combined output of firms S and C, we would be double-counting because we would be counting the steel used in the

Firm	Output
S	$100,000 steel
C	$ 75,000 chairs

manufacture of chairs twice. If firm C buys $25,000 of steel from firm S, we would subtract this amount from the value of C's output. By doing this, we would be using the *value-added* approach, and would thus avoid the problem of double-counting. The value-added approach entails adding only the values added by each firm. In our example, the value added by firm C would be $50,000.

The steel which firm C buys from firm S is an *intermediate product* which can be defined as an output of one firm which is used as an input by another firm. The finished product which is bought by the consumer is termed the *final product*. Double-counting can be avoided by counting only the value of the final products and excluding intermediate goods.

Secondly, in evaluating national income, we have to ensure that the income is a payment for goods and/or services produced. For example, if a university professor gives his son an allowance of $100 per month, it represents merely a *transfer* of income from one individual to another and would not constitute an addition to national income. If however, the professor pays $100 per month out of his salary to his part-time gardener, then it must be included in national income. The payment of $100 would then represent payment for gardening services provided.

Thirdly, a number of goods and services are produced but do not pass through the market. Examples of such goods and services are farm products grown by the farmer and consumed by him and his family, and room and board which a live-in housekeeper receives as a part of her salary. Since these represent goods and services actually produced, their values should be imputed.

THE COMPONENTS OF GNP

We noted that we could calculate the *GNP* by calculating the total expenditure on the total output. This can be done quite easily by adding up the expenditures of the various spending groups in the economy. The spending groups are:

1. Consumers whose spending we shall term consumption expenditures and which we shall denote by C.
2. Firms whose spending we shall term investment expendi-

tures. These purchases include expenditures on plant, equipment, buildings, etc.

3. Government whose purchases include payment for certain services such as health, education, etc., and payment for goods and services obtained from firms. Government expenditures will be denoted by G.

4. Foreigners whose expenditures constitute exports. We will denote exports by X. But we consume goods and services which we do not produce. These are called imports and are denoted by M. We have to subtract the imports from the exports. The resulting figure $(X - M)$ is termed net exports.

If we add all these components, we will obtain total expenditure denoted by E. Hence,

$$GNP \equiv E \equiv C + I + G + (X - M)$$

Table 5-1 shows the two approaches to the measurement of the national output.

Table 5-1. Canada's GNP for 1976 (in billions of dollars)

Factor Income Approach	Output Expenditure Approach
Wages, salaries and other labour income 109.10	Personal consumption expenditures (C) 110.54
Corporation profits before taxes less dividends paid to non-residents 18.37	Gross capital formation (I_g) 46.42
Net income from farm production and unincorporated business (including rent)........................ 11.76	Government expenditure on goods and services (G) 38.64
Interest and miscellaneous investment income.................. 10.63	Net exports (X - M) .... −4.71
Indirect taxes less subsidies 21.14	Residual error of estimate ...... −0.87
Capital consumption allowances and miscellaneous valuation adjustments (including inventory valuation adjustment).............................. 18.16	
Risidual error of estimate 0.87	
Total 190.03	Total 190.03

Source: Computed from Statistics Canada, National Income and Expenditure Accounts.

OTHER IMPORTANT ACCOUNTING CONCEPTS

The following are some other national income accounting concepts. *Depreciation.* During the year, the capital stock will have suffered some wearing out. This wear and tear of the capital stock is referred to as *depreciation* or *capital consumption*. If we subtract depreciation from *GNP*, we obtain a measure called *Net National Product (NNP)*. Thus if *D* represents depreciation, then

$$NNP = GNP - D$$

NNP is also referred to as *national income at market prices*.

The concepts of "gross" and "net" as applied to *GNP* and *NNP* apply also to investment. Gross investment (I_g) is the total investment made during the year without allowing for capital consumption. Gross investment is also known as *gross capital formation*. Net investment (I_n) is gross investment minus depreciation. It follows then that the investment component of *GNP* is gross investment whereas the investment component of *NNP* is net investment. Thus

$$GNP = C + I_g + G + (X - M)$$
$$NNP = C + I_n + G + (X - M)$$
$$I_g - I_n = D$$

Before payment is made to the factors of production out of the total output, *indirect business taxes* (T_{IB}) must be deducted. The resulting figure is known as *national income at factor cost*. This is the concept often referred to simply as *national income (NI)*. Thus

$$NI = NNP - T_{IB}$$

The entire national income is not distributed to factor owners as income. Certain deductions must be made. These include corporate taxes (T_c), undistributed profits (P_{un}), and social security payments *(SSP)*. On the other hand, people receive income in the form of unemployment compensation, old-age pensions, family allowances, etc. All such payments are called transfer payments *(TR)* and they form a part of *personal income (PI)* which we can define as income received from all sources. Thus

$$PI = NI - (T_c + P_{un} + SSP) + TR$$

The income earner pays taxes, and the part of his income that is left after personal income taxes (T_p) have been paid is called *disposable income (DI)*.

$$DI = PI - T_P$$

The relationships discussed above may be summarized as follows:

$$GNP - D = NNP$$
$$NNP - T_{IB} = NI$$
$$NI - (T_c + P_{un} + SSP) + TR = PI$$
$$PI - T_p = DI$$

The values of these measures for Canada in 1976 are given in Table 5-2.

Table 5-2. Relationship Between Various National Income Accounting Concepts for Canada, 1976.

($ billion)

Gross national product (GNP)	190.03
Capital consumption allowance (D) (including residual error of estimate)	− 21.05
Net National Product (NNP)	168.98
Indirect taxes less subsidies	− 21.14
National income (NI)	147.84
Corporate income taxes (T_c)	− 7.91
Undistributed corporation profits (P_{un})	− 7.66
Other earnings not paid out to persons	− 6.12
Government transfer payments (TR)	19.83
Interest on the public debt	7.97
Miscellaneous adjustments	1.85
Personal income (PI)	155.80
Personal taxes (T_p)	− 29.77
Disposable income (DI)	126.03

Source: Calculated from Statistics Canada, National Income and Expenditure Accounts.

CONSTANT VERSUS CURRENT DOLLARS: DEFLATING THE GNP

It will often be necessary to compare *GNP* (or some other accounting aggregate) of one country with that of another, or to compare the *GNP* of a country at one period with the *GNP* of the same country at a different period. The problem with such international and inter-temporal comparisons is that our measuring rod does not remain constant. Suppose we measure the *GNP* of a country in 1960 and 1970 and obtain values of $300 billion and $600 billion respectively. How useful will these figures be? Can we say, for example, that the country has produced twice as much in 1960 as it did in 1970? Before we can make such comparisons, we must first investigate the extent to which prices have changed.

The values given above are in *current dollars*, that is, the 1960 figure is quoted in 1960 dollars while the 1970 figure is quoted in 1970 dollars. If the value of the dollar has changed, the two figures given above are not comparable. The values must be expressed in the same units before direct comparison can take place. If prices have risen between 1960 and 1970, then the 1970 figure must be *deflated* to the 1960 level. After the deflation has taken place, the 1970 figure will be expressed in 1960 prices. The value obtained is called *real GNP*, and both values will be in *constant* (1960) dollars, rather than *current* (1960 and 1970) dollars.

If the values are expressed in 1960 dollars, then we may assign a value of 100 to the 1960 price level, and 1960 is said to be the *base year*. Let us assume that the statisticians have determined that in 1970, prices were 50% higher than they were in 1960. In this case, the 1970 price level would be given a value of 150. The numbers 100 and 150 are referred to as *price indices*. To deflate the 1970 *GNP*, we divide it by the 1970 price index. The price index is sometimes referred to as the *GNP deflator*. The process of deflation is illustrated in the following table.

Year	GNP (current $ billion)	GNP Price Index	Real GNP (constant 1960 $billion)
1960	300	100	$\dfrac{300 \times 100}{100} = 300.$
1970	600	150	$\dfrac{600 \times 100}{150} = 400.$

Table 5-3. Canada's GNP for Selected Years, 1950-1976

Year	GNP (current $ billion)	GNP (real 1971 $ billion)
1950	18.49	33.76
1955	28.53	43.89
1957	33.51	48.72
1960	38.36	53.23
1961	39.65	54.74
1962	42.93	58.48
1963	45.98	61.49
1964	50.28	65.61
1965	55.36	69.98
1966	61.83	74.84
1967	66.41	77.34
1968	72.59	81.86
1969	79.82	86.23
1970	85.69	88.39
1971	94.45	94.45
1972	105.23	100.25
1973	123.56	107.81
1974	147.18	111.77
1975	165.45	112.96
1976	190.03	118.48

Source: Statistics Canada, National Income and Expenditure Accounts.

Now that we have carried out the process of deflation, it is possible to compare the 1960 *GNP* with the 1970 *GNP*. The 1970 Gross National Product was only 1⅓ times the 1960 Gross National Product. Table 5-3 contains Canada's *GNP* in current and constant dollars for selected years from 1950 to 1976.

CHAPTER 6
INCOME DETERMINATION AND THE MULTIPLIER

Our task in this chapter is to find out what determines the level of national output. Throughout the analysis, we make the following assumptions: (1) the price level remains constant; (2) the economy has unemployed resources; and (3) the production possibility curve does not shift. We saw from the circular flow model, that injections and withdrawals determine the level of income in the circular flow. We can classify a number of economic variables either as injections or as withdrawals. The variables we will consider are saving (S), investment (I), government expenditure (G), taxes (T), exports (X), and imports (M).

Saving. We define saving as what is left out of income after expenditures on current consumption have been made. Consumers save when they decide not to spend their entire income on current consumption. If Y denotes income and C denotes consumption, then saving (S) may be expressed as follows:

$$S = Y - C$$

Saving is clearly a withdrawal from the circular flow.

Investment. We define investment as the production of capital goods. Capital goods are bought largely by firms to be used in the production of other goods. Machines are a good example of capital goods. Investment will increase the size of the circular flow and is therefore classified as an injection.

Government expenditure. The government produces certain goods and services such as police services, health services, schools, roads, etc. We will see in a later chapter that government expenditure (G) is an important variable in the macro-economy. Government expenditure is classified as an injection.

Taxes. The government imposes taxes on consumers and firms. When such taxes are imposed, income is taken out of the circular flow. Taxes are therefore classified as a withdrawal.

Exports. When a Canadian company exports goods to another country, the income of the Canadian company increases. If a British firm orders refrigerators from a Canadian manufacturer, the Canadian firm will require more factors of production to produce the additional refrigerators, hence the income of Canadian households will increase. It should be obvious from this example that exports inject income into the circular flow, hence they are classified as an injection.

Imports. When Canadians import goods, they spend income on goods produced by foreigners instead of Canadian firms. Income therefore flows out of the circular flow so we classify imports as a withdrawal.

The foregoing may be summarized in the following table of injections and withdrawals.

Injections (J)	Withdrawals (W)
Investment (I)	Saving (S)
Government spending (G)	Taxes (T)
Exports (X)	Imports (M)

Depending on the assumptions made, we can specify four different types of economies:
  (1) the simple economy without saving and investment
  (2) the economy with saving and investment
  (3) the economy with government
  (4) the economy with foreign trade, i.e., the open economy.
This classification, in fact, represents the various steps which we shall follow in developing a model of the economy which includes what we believe to be the most important determinants of the output of the economy as measured by national income figures. We shall begin first with a very simple model and, step by step, we shall introduce additional variables to make the model more useful.

EX ANTE AND EX POST QUANTITIES

It is important at this juncture to distinguish between actual or realized (ex post) quantities and planned or intended (ex ante) quantities. Failure to understand the distinction can lead to confusion. We will consider the ex ante and ex post concepts in terms of saving and investment. In an accounting sense, saving must always be equal to investment. This is so by definition. Realized (ex post) saving is income not spent on current consumption. Investment is the unconsumed part of current output. They are one and the same thing. This fact can be illustrated as follows. Let us assume that we are dealing with an economy consisting only of two sectors—households and firms. Total output and total income are identical and can be denoted by Y. Since total output consists of consumption and investment, we have

$$Y = C + I$$

Also, total income must either be consumed or saved, hence

$$Y = C + S$$

This implies that $C + S = C + I$

Therefore $S = I$

When we look at planned or intended (ex ante) saving and investment, we get a different picture. Whereas realized saving must equal realized investment (since they are the same thing), planned saving and planned investment are quite unlikely to be equal. Plans to save and plans to invest are made by different groups of people, and it is only by coincidence that they could be equal. In discussing equilibrium conditions, the relevant concepts are planned or ex ante quantities.

EQUILIBRIUM NATIONAL INCOME: INJECTIONS AND WITHDRAWALS

We will show how the equality of injections and withdrawals in each type of economy determines the equilibrium level of income.

Equilibrium in the simple economy without saving and investment. The simple economy without saving and investment is the economy which we studied in Chapter 5—the circular flow of income. There are neither injections nor withdrawals so the circular flow remains constant. The amount which people wish to spend is exactly equal to total output. The income is therefore an equilibrium level of income.

Equilibrium in the economy with saving and investment. In this economy, there are only two sectors—households and firms. We can simplify the analysis by assuming that all saving is done by households and investment is undertaken by firms. If intended investment is greater than intended saving (i.e., $J > W$), then income will tend to rise. If $S > I$, then income will tend to fall. If $S = I$, then income will be at its equilibrium level. We may state the equilibrium condition for the economy with saving and investment as follows:

The economy with saving and investment will be in equilibrium when intended saving equals intended investment.

Equilibrium in the economy with government. We now add the government sector to our economy. This gives us two more variables (G and T) to consider. In this economy, total injection is the sum of investment (I) and government expenditure (G). Total withdrawal is the sum of saving (S) and taxes (T).

If $(I + G) > (S + T)$, then income will tend to rise.

If $(I + G) < (S + T)$, then income will tend to fall.

If $(I + G) = (S + T)$, then income will remain constant.

The economy with a government sector will be in equilibrium when the sum of investment and government spending is equal to the sum of saving and taxes.

Equilibrium in the open economy. The opening up of our economy to foreign trade has added two new variables—exports and imports. Total injection now consists of investment, government spending, and exports (X). Total withdrawal consists of saving, taxes, and imports (M).

If $(I + G + X) > (S + T + M)$, then income will tend to rise.

If $(I + G + X) < (S + T + M)$, then income will tend to fall.

If $(I + G + X) = (S + T + M)$, then income will remain constant.

The open economy will be in equilibrium when the sum of investment, government spending, and exports, is equal to the sum of saving, taxes, and imports.

EQUILIBRIUM NATIONAL INCOME: A GRAPHICAL ANALYSIS

We can illustrate equilibrium in the economy with saving and investment by using the following saving-investment figure.

We assume that saving varies directly with income. As income increases, saving increases; and as income falls, saving falls. This relationship between saving and income is called the *saving function* and can be written as $S = S(Y)$. Note that saving becomes positive only after income has reached to a certain level (beyond Y_0 in the figure). Below Y_0, saving is negative. When saving is negative, we say that people are *dissaving*. We assume that investment is *autonomous*, i.e., it does not vary with changes in income. We show this by drawing investment as a horizontal line as shown in Figure 6.1. Income will be in equilibrium where saving is equal to investment—i.e., at the income level $\overline{Y}$.

We turn now to a different approach to the determination of equilibrium national income. *Aggregate demand* (AD) is total expenditure.

FIG. 6-1

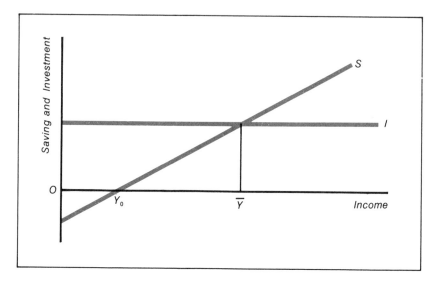

The components of aggregate demand depends on the type of economy we are studying. In the economy with only households and firms, aggregate demand is the sum of consumption and investment. That is,

$AD = C + I$

In the economy with government, aggregate demand is the sum of consumption, investment and government spending. That is,

$AD = C + I + G$

In the open economy, aggregate demand is the sum of consumption, investment, government spending and spending by foreigners (net exports). Thus for the open economy we have

$AD = C + I + G + (X - M)$

Equilibrium in the simple economy without saving and investment.

We assume that consumption varies directly with income. If income increases, consumption increases; and if income decreases, consumption falls. This relationship between consumption and income is called the *consumption function*, and can be written as $C = C(Y)$. Figure 6-2 is a graphical representation of the consumption function. We shall return, in a later chapter to a more detailed analysis of consumption behaviour.

Note that the consumption function cuts the vertical axis at a positive value. This implies that some consumption takes place even at a zero level of income.

The construction of a 45° line as shown in Figure 6-3 is important

FIG. 6-2

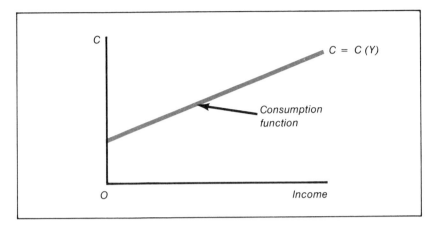

FIG. 6-3

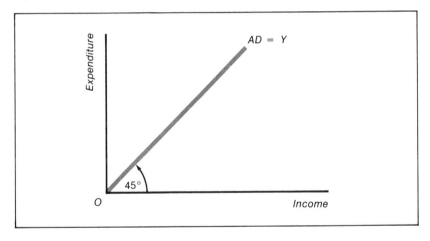

in the graphical analysis. At each point on the 45° line, expenditure is equal to income.

In Figure 6-4, consumption is the only component of aggregate demand, therefore $AD = C$. At $\overline{Y}_1$, expenditure generated by that level of income is less than total output. The firms will be unable to sell their entire output and would therefore reduce production, causing income to fall. At $\overline{Y}_0$, planned expenditure is greater than total output. The firms will observe that their output is insufficient to satisfy consumers and would therefore increase production, causing income to rise. It is only at $\overline{Y}$ that planned expenditure is exactly equal to total output. At this level,

FIG. 6-4

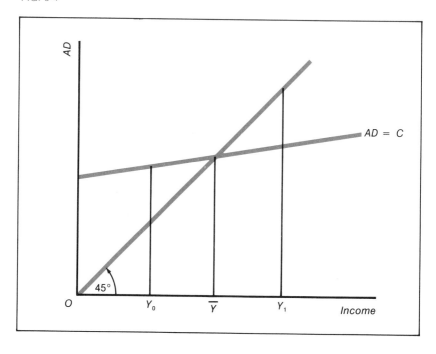

there is no tendency for income to rise or fall. $\overline{Y}$ is therefore the equilibrium level of income.

Equilibrium in the economy with saving and investment. We have already used the saving-investment diagram to illustrate equilibirum in the economy with saving and investment. We shall now use the aggregate demand diagram to illustrate the same idea. Total expenditure in this economy consists of consumption and investment. We assume, as before, that investment is autonomous. In Figure 6-5, the expenditure function $C + I$ is shown above the consumption function.

The equilibrium level of income is $\overline{Y}$ where total intended spending by households and firms is exactly equal to total output. As an exercise, the student should verify that any other level of income cannot be an equilibrium level.

Equilibrium in the economy with government. We assume that government expenditure (G) is also autonomous. In Figure 6-6, aggregate demand is shown now as $C + I + G$.

The economy with a government sector will be in equilibrium when

FIG. 6-5

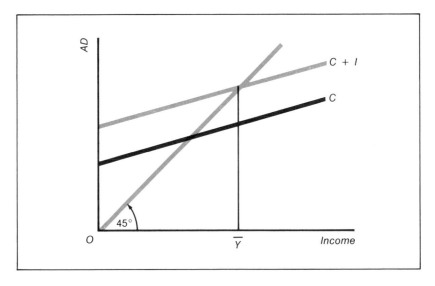

FIG. 6-6

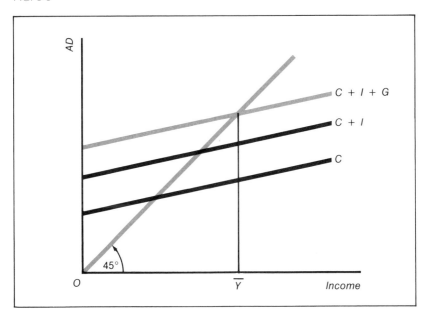

total planned spending $(C + I + G)$ is equal to total output. This occurs at a level of income indicated by $\overline{Y}$. The student is again advised to verify that any level of income other than $\overline{Y}$ cannot be an equilibrium level.

FIG. 6-7

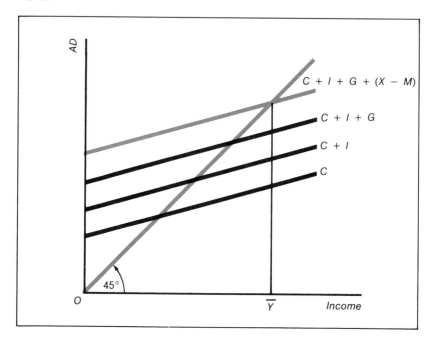

Equilibrium in the open economy.

Net exports $(X - M)$ are treated as autonomous in this model. Aggregate demand is now $C + I + G + (X - M)$. The aggregate demand function for the open economy is shown in Figure 6-7.

The equilibrium level of income in this economy is $\overline{Y}$ where total desired spending is equal to total output.

INCOME CHANGES AND THE MULTIPLIER

Let us consider the economy with saving and investment. We wish to investigate the effect on equilibrium income of a change in investment.

The effect of an increase in investment.

Let us first look at the effect of an increase in investment. In Figure 6-8, I_1 is the original level of investment. The equilibrium level of income is $\overline{Y}_1$. An increase in investment is shown by shifting the investment line upward as shown in the figure by I_2.

Given the saving function, the new equilibrium level of income is now $\overline{Y}_2$ which is greater than $\overline{Y}_1$. We have therefore seen that an increase in

FIG. 6-8

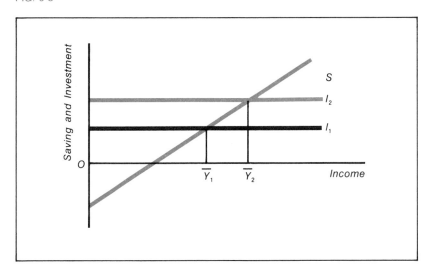

investment, other things being equal, will increase the equilibrium level of income. The effect of a decrease in investment is left as an exercise for the student.

The effects of an increase in saving.   In the following diagram, the equilibrium level of income is $\overline{Y}_1$ where saving equals investment. An increase in saving is shown by shifting the saving function upward from S_1 to S_2 as shown in Figure 6-9. Given the level of investment, the increase in saving results in a lower level of equilibrium income as shown by the movement from $\overline{Y}_1$ to $\overline{Y}_0$

The fact that an increase in saving actually diminishes national income is called the *paradox of thrift*. It is called a paradox because whereas saving is considered to be good from the individual's point of view (he will be better off in the future), it is bad for the economy as a whole, since total income actually falls in the future. Also, as the level of national income falls, the level of saving will also fall. Thus it turns out (paradoxically) that if households attempt to increase their saving, aggregate saving will decrease.

THE MULTIPLIER

In order to study the multiplier, we must introduce a few new concepts.

FIG. 6-9

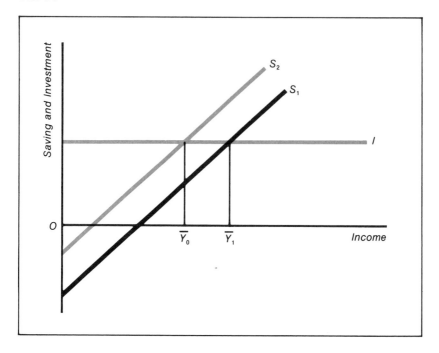

The average propensity to consume (APC).

The average propensity to consume is the ratio of total consumption to total income. That is,

$$APC = \frac{C}{Y}$$

For example, if total income is $500 million and consumption expenditures amount to $400 million, then

$$APC = \frac{C}{Y} = \frac{400}{500} = 0.8$$

The marginal propensity to consume (MPC).

The marginal propensity to consume is defined as the change in consumption resulting from a change in income. It is the fraction of extra income that is devoted to consumption. Using " Δ " to denote "a change in", we can express the MPC as

$$MPC = \frac{\Delta C}{\Delta Y}$$

For example, if income increases from \$500 million to \$600 million and consumption increases from \$400 million to \$480 million, then

$$MPC = \frac{\Delta C}{\Delta Y} = \frac{480 - 400}{600 - 500} = \frac{80}{100} = 0.8$$

The average propensity to save (APS).   The average propensity to save is total saving divided by total income. That is,

$$APS = \frac{S}{Y}$$

The marginal propensity to save (MPS).   The marginal propensity to save is the fraction of extra income devoted to saving. It is defined as the change in saving divided by the change in income. That is,

$$MPS = \frac{\Delta S}{\Delta Y}$$

If the MPC is ¾, then the MPS is ¼. It should be obvious that $MPC + MPS = 1$.

We noted that an increase in investment will increase income. By how much will income increase when investment increases? To answer this question, we must turn to the multiplier. The *multiplier* is the ratio of the change in income to the change in expenditure which generates the change in income. If we use k to denote the multiplier, and if the change in expenditure is a change in investment (ΔI), then

$$k = \frac{\Delta Y}{\Delta I}$$

The following example will illustrate how the multiplier works. Suppose the MPC is 0.5. An expenditure of \$400 million will become income to those who receive it. The recipients will in turn spend ½ of the \$400 million, and so on. The process is illustrated in the table below.

The process continues until additional income generated becomes almost zero. It is obvious that the total income generated will be several times the increase in the initial expenditure. The value of the multiplier can be determined by applying the formula

$$k = \frac{1}{1 - MPC} = \frac{1}{MPS} \text{ where } k \text{ is the multiplier.}$$

Expenditure ($billion)	Income generated ($billion)
400	400
½ of 400 200	200
½ of 200 100	100
½ of 100 50	50
½ of 50 25	25
„	„
„	„

In the above arithmetic example, since the $MPC = \frac{1}{2}$.

$$k = \frac{1}{1 - \frac{1}{2}} = \frac{1}{\frac{1}{2}} = 2.$$

The new level of income will be $\Delta Y = k \, \Delta I$
$$= 2 \times 400 = 800.$$

Example. Given an MPC of 0.8, find the increase in income resulting from an increase in investment from \$80 million to \$140 million.

The change in investment, $\Delta I = 140 - 80 = 60$.

$$\text{The multiplier } k = \frac{1}{1 - MPC} = \frac{1}{1 - \frac{4}{5}} = \frac{1}{\frac{1}{5}} = 5.$$

$$\Delta Y = k \, \Delta I$$
$$= 5 \times 60 = 300.$$

The increase in income will therefore be \$300 million.

NOTE: The change in expenditure that we have been considering is a change in investment. But the change in expenditure could have been a change in any expenditure item such as G, for example.

A graphical representation.   The multiplier can also be represented graphically. In Figure 6-10, an increase in investment from I_1 to I_2 has caused income to increase from $\overline{Y}_1$ to $\overline{Y}_2$.

The multiplier is $\frac{\Delta Y}{\Delta I}$.

The value of the multiplier.   The Figure shows that the change in income is greater than the change in spending which generates the change. This implies that the multiplier is positive and greater than one. Let us investigate this further. We assume that if people receive extra income, they will consume a part,

FIG. 6-10

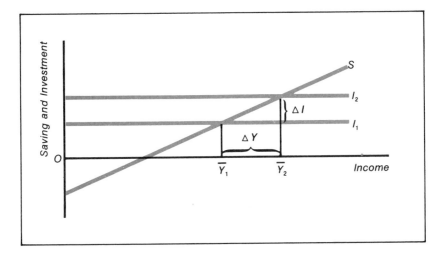

but not all, of it. Hence the *MPC* is a positive fraction. This may be expressed as follows:

$$0 < MPC < 1.$$

If the *MPC* is a positive fraction, the *MPS* is also a positive fraction, hence

$$0 < MPS < 1.$$

But the multiplier k is $\dfrac{1}{1 - MPC} = \dfrac{1}{MPS}$.

Since the *MPS* is a positive fraction, then its inverse must be greater than 1. The multiplier is therefore greater than 1.

We have looked at the multiplier for an economy in which the only withdrawal is saving. In reality, however, withdrawals consist of savings, imports and taxes. When these other withdrawals are taken into account, the value of the multiplier will be different. In general, the multiplier will be the reciprocal of the marginal propensity to withdraw (*MPW*). The *MPW* is the fraction of extra income devoted to saving, imports and taxes. That is,

$$MPW = \frac{\Delta W}{\Delta Y,} \text{ and } k = \frac{1}{MPW}$$

We are now in a position to use this simple model to get a rough estimate of the multiplier for Canada.

From 1975 to 1976, Canada's *GNP* increased from $165.45 billion to $190.03 billion, an increase of $24.58 billion. The increase in withdrawals

Estimate of Canada's Multiplier, 1975-76

($billion)

	GNP	W	$\triangle$ GNP	$\triangle$ W	$MPW = \dfrac{\triangle W}{\triangle GNP}$
1975	165.45	136.55			
1976	190.03	151.00	24.48	14.45	0.59

was $14.45 billion. This gives a marginal propensity to withdraw of 0.59.

$$\text{Since } MPW = 0.59$$
$$k = \frac{1}{0.59} = 1.69.$$

A rough estimate for Canda's multiplier is therefore 1.69.

THE INFLATIONARY AND DEFLATIONARY GAPS

Up to this point, we have assumed that the price level is constant and that the economy has unemployed resources. If planned expenditure exceeds total output, total output expands until equilibrium is reached. If aggregate demand falls short of total output, output contracts until the two are equal. Now let us change the assumption of unemployed resources and assume that the economy is operating on its production possibility curve. It is necessary also to drop the assumption of constant prices.

The inflationary gap.   If aggregate demand is greater than full-employment output, prices will tend to rise. This is referred to as an inflationary situation. The excess of aggregate demand over full-employment output is called the *inflationary gap*. In Figure 6-11, Y_f represents full-employment output or *potential output*, a term also used.

GF represents the inflationary gap—the amount by which aggregate demand exceeds full-employment output.

The deflationary gap.   If aggregate demand falls short of full-employment output, real output will tend to fall. This is referred to as a deflationary situation. The amount by which aggregate demand falls short of full-employment output is the *deflationary gap*. The term deflation actually means falling prices. But if a deflationary gap exists, prices may remain fairly

FIG. 6-11

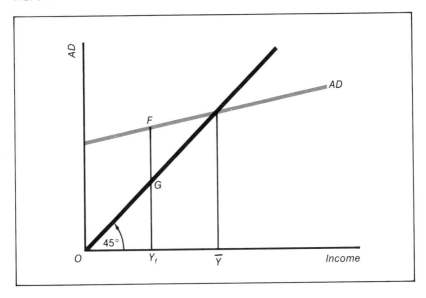

FIG. 6-12

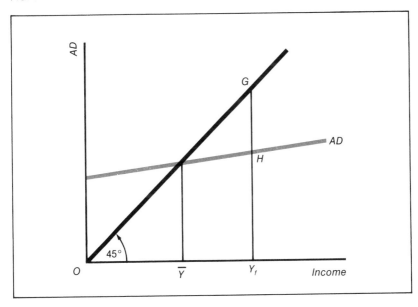

steady but there will be unemployment. Figure 6-12 illustrates the deflationary gap.

At full-employment output, Y_f, aggregate demand falls short of the full-employment output by GH. GH represents the deflationary gap.

CHAPTER 7
THE CONSUMPTION FUNCTION

The theory of consumption which we are about to study now is the Keynesian theory. The theory was developed by J.M. Keynes in his revolutionary book, *The General Theory of Employment, Interest and Money*, published in 1936. We assume that consumption changes directly with current income. According to Keynes, if income increases, consumption will increase but not by as much as the increase in income. This he refers to as a *fundamental psychological law*. This tells us that the *MPC* is greater than zero but less than one. If the *MPC* is constant, the consumption function will be linear as shown in Figure 7-1A below. If the *MPC* declines, then the consumption function will have the shape indicated in Figure 7-1B.

A declining *MPC* implies that the increase in consumption decreases with successive increases in income. Table 7-1 contains data on disposable income and consumption expenditure for Canada from 1960 to 1976.

FIG. 7-1A, 7-1B

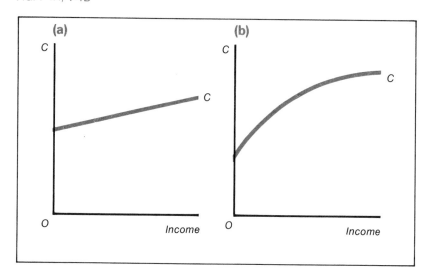

A movement along the consumption function vs a shift in the consumption function.

The distinction between a movement along the same consumption function and a shift in the consumption function is similar to the distinction made between a movement along a demand curve and a shift in the demand curve (Figs. 3-2, 3-3). In Figure 7-2, if current income increases from Y_1 to Y_2, consumption will increase from C_1 to C_2. This is a movement along the consumption function. If however, consumption increases for any reason other than an increase in current income, then there will be a shift in the consumption function from C to C^*. At any level of income, more will be consumed.

FIG. 7-2

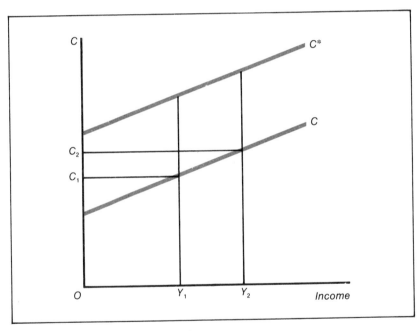

THE DETERMINANTS OF CONSUMPTION

Current income is obviously one of the most important factors affecting consumption. Other factors likely to influence consumption are interest rates, price expectations, income distribution, and the terms of credit.

Table 7-1. Disposable Income and Consumption, Canada 1960-76

($billion)

Year	Disposable Income	Consumption
1960	26.57	25.48
1961	26.90	25.93
1962	29.34	27.45
1963	31.17	29.23
1964	33.05	31.39
1965	36.26	33.95
1966	39.90	36.89
1967	43.12	39.97
1968	46.82	43.70
1969	50.91	47.49
1970	54.01	50.33
1971	59.94	55.62
1972	68.10	62.21
1973	79.72	71.28
1974	94.73	83.44
1975	111.13	97.02
1976	126.03	110.54

Source: Statistics Canada, National Income and Expenditure Accounts.

Interest rates. If the rate of interest increases, people may save more. A larger volume of saving implies a smaller volume of consumption. An increase in the rate of interest may therefore cause the consumption function to shift downward. The effect of changes in the rate of interest on consumption may be viewed in another way. Consumers generally borrow to purchase certain commodities, particularly durable consumer goods such as furniture and appliances. High interest rates may deter them from borrowing and thus reduce expenditure on these goods. Low interest rates, on the other hand, will tend to increase consumption.

Price expectations. Expectations of price changes can affect consumption expenditures. If households expect prices to rise, they are likely to increase their expenditures to avoid higher prices in the future. On the other hand, if they expect prices to fall, they are likely to postpone consumption in order to take advantage of the lower prices in the future.

Income distribution. A change in the distribution of income is likely to have some effect on consumption. If people with lower incomes have larger *MPCs* than people with higher incomes, then a redistribution of income from people with higher incomes to those with lower incomes will increase total consumption spending.

The terms of credit. If goods are available on easy credit terms, then consumption expenditures are likely to be higher than in a situation where it is difficult to obtain credit. If a TV set can be obtained with a small downpayment, consumers need not postpone consumption until they can "save up" the full amount to pay for the set.

OTHER THEORIES OF THE CONSUMPTION FUNCTION

So far, we have related consumption to current income. It has been argued that past income is extremely important in explaining current consumption. According to this theory, changes in current income may not have any significant effect on current consumption. Consumers may have established a certain pattern of consumption based on previous income levels. If current income falls, they will try to maintain their current level of consumption by borrowing or by reducing their accumulated savings. Similarly, if current income rises, it may take a while for consumers to adjust to the higher level of consumption made possible as a result of the higher income.

The Permanent Income Hypothesis. The Permanent Income Hypothesis advanced by Professor Milton Friedman is a popular alternative theory of the consumption function. This theory states that *permanent income* has a greater influence on consumption than does current income. Permanent income may be regarded as average expected lifetime income. According to this theory, a graduate student may consume more than his current income now because he expects a much higher income stream in the future. So too, a household that wins a lottery will not suddenly increase consumption significantly, but will attempt to "even out" consumption by spreading it over a long period of time.

The permanent income hypothesis implies that attempts to influence consumption by changing current income will fail unless such changes are viewed as permanent. A tax reduction this year which is not expected to continue in the future will not, according to this theory, do much to stimulate consumption spending.

CHAPTER 8

INVESTMENT AND THE ACCELERATION PRINCIPLE

Gross National Product fluctuates from time to time. These ups and downs in the economy are referred to as the *business cycle* or *business fluctuations*. Figure 8-1 illustrates these cyclical fluctuations.

FIG. 8-1

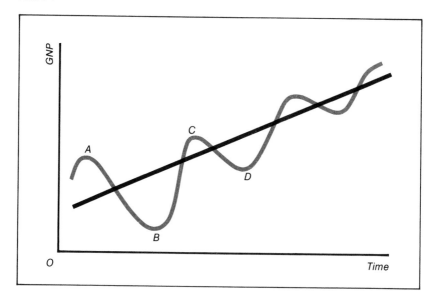

Economists use the term *depression* to refer to a severe fall in output and employment. Point *B* in the diagram illustrates such a situation. If the fall in output and employment is a mild one, the term recession is used.

When the economy is recovering from a depression or a recession, output and employment increase. This is known as a period of *recovery* or *expansion* and is illustrated by a move from *B* towards *C* which is called the *peak* of the cycle. If there is a persistent rise in the price level as the peak is reached, the economy is said to be in an *inflation*.

One of the major causes of fluctuations in *GNP* is changes in investment. It is important therefore to know why investment is such a volatile element of aggregate demand. The components of investment

52

are investment in inventories; business fixed investment (i.e., investment in machinery, plant and equipment); and investment in housing. Business fixed investment is the largest component of investment but it appears to be the most stable. Investment in inventories and investment in housing are therefore the two components which have earned investment the fame of being the most volatile element of aggregate demand.

In the models that we have developed so far, we have treated investment as given. We will now change that assumption and consider some of the factors likely to affect investment. We shall consider only the following: (1) investment as a function of the rate of interest, (2) investment as a function of expectations, (3) investment as a function of retained earnings, and (4) investment as a function of changes in national income. The relationship between investment and changes in national income is often referred to as the *accelerator theory*. We will consider each of these theories in turn.

The rate of interest.   It is generally believed by economists that there is an inverse relationship between the level of investment and the rate of interest. The production of capital goods often requires borrowed funds. The higher the rate of interest, the higher will be the cost of borrowing. The lower the rate of interest, the lower the cost of borrowing. This implies that, other things being equal, high interest rates will discourage borrowing and hence investment, whereas low interest rates will encourage borrowing and therefore stimulate investment.

This inverse relationship between investment and the rate of interest is usually summed up in the *marginal efficiency of investment schedule*. Figure 8-2 shows a marginal efficiency of investment schedule.

The figure shows that a fall in the rate of interest from r_1 to r_0 causes investment to increase from I_0 to I_1.

The effect of a change in the rate of interest depends on the slope of the marginal efficiency of investment schedule. In Figure 8-3A below, a fall in the interest rate from r_1 to r_0 causes only a small increase in investment, from I_0 to I_1. This is because the marginal efficiency of investment (MEI) schedule is so steep. In Figure 8-3B, the slope is less and the fall in the rate of interest causes a much larger increase in investment (from I_2 to I_3).

Expectations.   Business expectations about the future can be subject to a high degree of variability. The volatility of investment is sometimes blamed on the variability of business expectations. If businessmen look to the future with optimism, there is likely to be a higher level of investment than would otherwise be the case. If, for example, businessmen expect a

FIG. 8-2

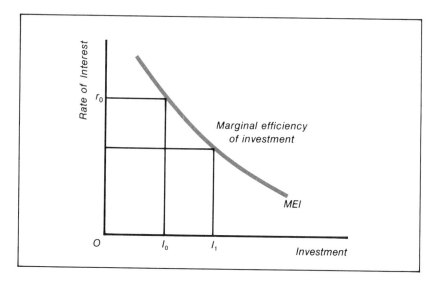

FIG. 8-3A, 8-3B

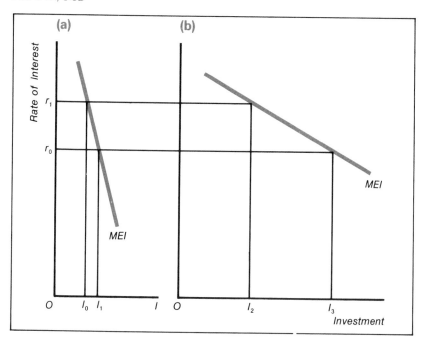

sustained increase in *GNP* and hence in total consumption, they are
likely to increase their capital stock to be able to meet the higher level
of demand. Of course, the increase in investment will itself help to

increase *GNP* so that the expectation becomes somewhat self-fulfilling. If, on the other hand, businessmen expect a gloomy future, they are unlikely to engage in investment activities.

It is conceivable that a pessimistic forecast may even delay replacement investment. This "run down" in the capital stock is referred to as *disinvestment*.

Retained earnings. Borrowing is only one source of funds for investment purposes. Firms often withhold a part of their earnings rather than distributing it among their shareholders. These *retained earnings* are a source of investment funds. Other things being equal, one can expect the level of investment to vary directly with the volume of retained earnings.

The acceleration principle. The acceleration theory of investment was introduced into the body of economic knowledge in 1917 by J.M. Clark. According to this theory, investment is a function of the rate of change of income. If income is increasing, consumption will also be increasing. There will be an increase in demand for capital goods to produce consumer goods so investment increases. On the other hand, if income is falling, consumption will also be falling, and therefore investment is likely to fall also.

The following algebraic formulation of the accelerator theory may be useful. We define the *capital-output* ratio as the amount of capital required to produce a unit of the annual output. If K denotes capital, and Y denotes annual output, then the capital-output ratio is given by $\dfrac{K}{Y}$. We assume that this ratio is constant and denote it by v. Hence

$$v = \frac{K}{Y} \tag{1}$$

The concept of investment which we shall use is net investment (I_n), i.e., an addition to the capital stock. Therefore

$$I_n = \Delta K \tag{2}$$

From (1) we obtain

$$K = vY \tag{3}$$

$$\text{Therefore } \Delta K = v \ \Delta Y$$

$$\text{But } \Delta K = I_n$$

$$\text{Therefore } I_n = v \Delta Y.$$

Thus, given a capital-output ratio of 4:1, an increase in income of $10 billion will cause investment to increase by $40 billion. That is, the change in investment will be proportionately greater than the increase in demand which induced it.

The accelerator theory implies that output must continually increase for investment to take place. A reduction in the rate of change of output will cause investment to fall off. The theory also implies that investment responds fairly readily to changes in demand brought about by changes in income. But in reality, firms are unlikely to adjust their capital stock so readily to changes in demand. If excess capacity exists, the firms will use this excess capacity to increase output. If excess capacity is zero, the firms may use their existing plants overtime.

Interaction of the accelerator and the multiplier. Professor Paul Samuelson developed a model in which he shows how the accelerator and the multiplier interact to produce cumulative changes in *GNP*. Only a highly simplified version of the model can be presented here. Consider a situation where the economy is experiencing high unemployment. Suppose businessmen expect an increase in demand in the future. To be able to meet the increase in demand for consumer goods and services, new investment is made. The increase in investment causes an increase in income via the multiplier. This increase in income leads to an increase in demand for capital goods and hence to new investment. The process can be illustrated with the help of the following figure.

FIG. 8-4

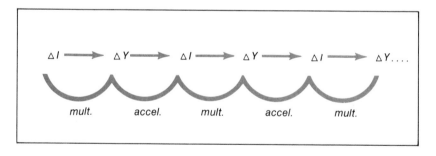

The original stimulus comes from an increase in investment. This increases income which increases investment which increases income and so on. The process can also work in reverse. If investment falls because of a pessimistic business outlook, the multiplier-accelerator process can produce a cumulative downward movement in income.

This multiplier-accelerator model implies that fluctuations in income and employment can be long lasting and severe unless policies are adopted to counteract these changes.

CHAPTER 9
FISCAL POLICY

Fiscal policy may be defined as changes in government spending (G) and/or taxes (T) designed to influence income and employment. Government spending is a relatively large component of aggregate demand. It follows that changes in government spending can change aggregate spending and therefore affect income and employment. In this chapter, we shall study the effects of government spending and taxation on the level of output and employment. Any attempt to regulate aggregate demand in order to promote full employment without inflation is stabilization policy. Fiscal policy is therefore one aspect of stabilization policy.

If government expenditure is equal to tax revenues, the government is said to have a *balanced budget*. If government expenditure is greater than tax revenues, there is a *budget deficit*, and if government expenditure is less than its tax revenues, then there is a *budget surplus*. The government engages in *deficit financing* when it increases its spending without raising taxes. If the government increases its spending while at the same time increasing taxes by the same amount, we refer to it as a *balanced budget increase in spending*.

The government can engage in deficit financing only by borrowing. There are three main sources from which the government can borrow. It can borrow from the public by issuing bonds, it can borrow from the central bank, and it can borrow from the banking system. The government incurs a debt by borrowing, and it has to pay interest on its loan. There is a great deal of talk about the national debt. Below, we will attempt to determine whether the concern over the national debt is justified.

FISCAL POLICY AS A MEASURE AGAINST UNEMPLOYMENT

Let us assume that a deflationary gap exists in the economy. Here we have a situation where total spending is insufficient to purchase full-employment output. The problem is a deficiency of aggregate demand. In the Figure 9-1, we assume that we are dealing with a closed economy, i.e., an economy without a foreign sector.

The economy is in equilibrium at a level of income of $\overline{Y}$ which is below the full-employment level. At the full-employment level of

FIG. 9-1

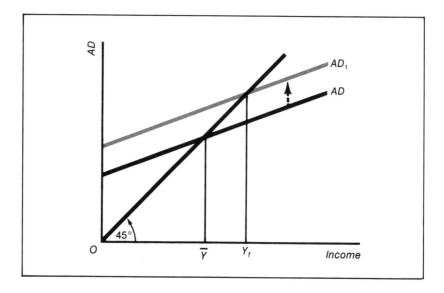

income, aggregate demand falls short of total expenditure. To have equilibrium at full employment, the aggregate demand function must shift upward from *AD* to *AD*₁ as shown in the diagram. This shift in aggregate demand will eliminate the deflationary gap.

The appropriate fiscal policy in this situation is an increase in government spending or a reduction in taxes. In other words, a deficit in the budget is required. An increase in government spending will increase income and employment. The increase in income will cause consumption to increase. The increase in consumption may cause investment to increase as we saw from the accelerator theory of investment. This increase in investment will cause income to increase via the multiplier. We note that all components of aggregate demand increase as a result of the increase in government spending, hence the entire aggregate demand function shifts upward.

Similarly, a reduction in taxes increases disposable income. The increase in disposable income generates an increase in consumption and possibly an increase in investment as we outlined above. Again, aggregate demand shifts upward. Fiscal policy aimed at increasing aggregate demand is said to be *expansionary*.

FISCAL POLICY TO REDUCE INFLATION

Let us now assume that an inflationary gap exists. The situation is illustrated in Figure 9-2.

FIG. 9-2

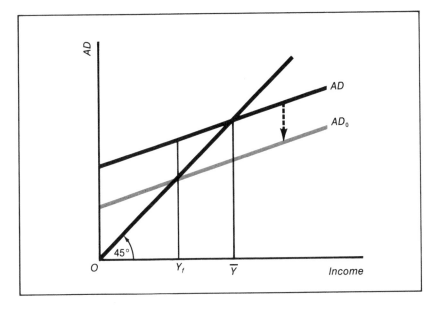

Again, we assume a closed economy so that the components of aggregate demand are C, I, and G. Aggregate demand is now greater than full-employment output so the level of prices will rise. What is needed here is a reduction of aggregate demand from AD to AD_0 to eliminate the inflationary gap.

The appropriate fiscal policy to reduce aggregate demand is a reduction in government spending and an increase in taxes—i.e., a budget surplus. A decrease in government spending reduces income. As income falls, consumption and possibly investment will fall. An increase in taxes reduces disposable income and hence consumption. Investment may also fall as a result. These changes produce the desired downward shift in the expenditure function to eliminate the deflationary gap. Fiscal policy designed to reduce aggregate demand is termed *contractionary fiscal policy*. The type of deliberate fiscal policy that we have been discussing is often called *discretionary fiscal policy* to distinguish it from *automatic fiscal policy* or *non-discretionary fiscal policy* to which we now turn.

Automatic (built-in) stabilizers. There are certain fiscal policy measures that have been built into our economic system. These measures ensure that government spending and taxes change automatically as income and employment fluctuate.

Unemployment compensation and agricultural subsidies are two examples of built-in stabilizers. When unemployment is rising and national income is falling, government expenditure in the form of unemployment compensation increases. This injection into the economy will have a stimulating effect on income and employment. If the economy is in an inflationary situation with income rising, the demand for agricultural products will increase. Other things being equal, the prices of agricultural products will rise and the need for subsidies will fall as the income of farmers increases. The foregoing implies that the built-in stabilizers help to increase aggregate demand when income and employment are low and to reduce total spending in inflationary situations.

But a built-in stabilizer may work in a perverse manner. For example, if the economy is in a recession, the government may attempt to stimulate aggregate demand by increasing government spending. The increase in government spending will increase income. But when income increases, tax receipts also increase, and this may have a contractionary effect on the economy. This built-in stabilizer which prevents the economy from recovering from a slump is called the *fiscal drag*. In the example that we have given, a tax cut may be necessary to counteract the effect of the fiscal drag.

THE PUBLIC DEBT

There is often a great deal of debate on the issue of the public debt. The *public debt* or the *national debt* as it is often called is simply the government's indebtedness to the people. If the government owes the people $250 billion, it can settle its debt by raising taxes by $250 billion and paying off its debt with the proceeds. It simply takes the money from the people and returns it to them. This action would redistribute income but would not affect total income. Many people have expressed earnest fears that the government may go bankrupt because of the massive size of the public debt. The public debt is indeed large in an absolute sense, but the size of the public debt is better understood if it is discussed with reference to some other magnitude such as the *GNP*. Table 9-1 shows that the rather large absolute size of the fedral public debt ($41.3 billion in 1976), represents only 22 percent of *GNP*. Moreover, the federal public debt as a percentage of *GNP* has fallen steadily over the past several years. It is clear that this danger is imaginary rather than real if the debt is owed to residents of the country. If however, the debt is owed to foreigners, then payment must be made by transferring goods from the borrowing to the lending country. In this case, there will be a real reduction in the amount of goods available in the country.

The table shows that only a very small percentage (5.8%) of the

Table 9-1. The Significance of the Public Debt, Canada 1976

Public debt held by Canadian institutions and the Canadian public	$38.90 billion
Public debt held by Canadians as a % of total public debt	94.2%
Public debt held by non-residents	$2.4 billion
Public debt held by non-residents as a % of total public debt	5.8%
Total Federal public debt	$41.30 billion
Public debt as a % of GNP	22%
Interest payments	$4.52 billion
Interest payment as % of GNP	2.4%

Sources: Computed from Bank of Canada Review, and Statistics Canada, National Income and Expenditure Accounts.

federal public debt is owed to non-residents. Annual interest payment on the public debt has also caused considerable concern. Interest payment as a percentage of *GNP* has not changed drastically over the past years, and in 1976, interest charges on the debt amounted to $4.5 billion or approximately 2.4 percent of the *GNP* (see Table 9-1).

THE BALANCED BUDGET MULTIPLIER

Consider a situation where there is unemployment in the economy. The government may increase its spending and at the same time raise taxes to finance the increase in spending. It may be thought that this balanced budget will have no effect on total income. But it can be demonstrated that a given increase in government expenditure financed by an equivalent increase in taxes, will increase equilibrium income by the amount of the government spending. This is what is often termed the *balanced budget theorem* and it asserts that the balanced budget multiplier is unity. The following example illustrates the implication of the balanced budget theorem. Let us assume that the *MPC* is 0.8. If government expenditure increases by $6 billion, income will increase by $30 billion (since the multiplier will be 5). For the simple Keynesian model that we have been studying, it can be shown that the government multiplier (k_g) is always greater than the tax multiplier (k_t) by 1. That is, $k_g - k_t = 1$.

Thus, in our numerical example, since the government multiplier is 5, the tax multiplier is 4. Therefore, if taxes rise by $6 billion, income will decline by $24 billion leaving a net increase of $6 billion. Another example using a different value for the *MPC* and a different value for the increase in government spending will yield the same result that the balanced budget multiplier is unity. Assume an *MPC* of $\frac{5}{7}$. This means that $k_g = \dfrac{1}{1 - \dfrac{5}{7}} = \dfrac{1}{\dfrac{2}{7}} = \dfrac{7}{2}.$ An increase in government spending of

$14 billion will therefore increase income by $49 billion. The tax multiplier in this case will be $\dfrac{7}{2} - 1 = \dfrac{5}{2}.$ A tax increase of $14 billion will therefore decrease income by $35 billion. The net increase in income is $14 billion which again is equal to the increase in government spending.

An issue which is closely related to the balanced budget multiplier concerns the relative stimulative effects of an increase in government spending and a reduction of taxes of the same magnitude. An increase in government spending of $50 million is a direct injection of that amount into the economy. On the other hand, a $50 million reduction in taxes puts the extra disposable income into the hands of people who may not spend it all on domestically produced goods and services.

The permanent income hypothesis which we studied earlier has something to add to this discussion. If people regard tax reductions as a temporary measure to stimulate the economy, the permanent income theory of the consumption function predicts that consumption will not respond significantly to such "transitory" income changes. The implication is that a tax reduction may not have a very expansionary effect on income and employment.

CHAPTER 10
MONETARY THEORY

Money is certainly the most discussed and probably the most misunderstood aspect of the economy. So far, we have not paid any special attention to money per se. In this chapter, and in the next two chapters, we shall look at the functions of money, banking activities, the control of the money supply, and the effect of money on the economy.

Definition of money. Money is defined as anything that is generally accepted as payment for goods and services. Before the invention of money, one good had to be exchanged directly for another good. This is commonly known as *barter*. Under a system of barter, if one man has shoes which he wants to exchange for meat, he would have to find somebody who has meat and who wants to exchange it for shoes. Exchange under this system therefore requires a *double coincidence of wants*. Needless to say, this system is very time-consuming. Because money is generally acceptable, it eliminates the need for a double coincidence of wants. A trader exchanges his goods for money, and with the money, he purchases the goods and services he requires.

The functions of money. Money performs three main functions. It serves as a medium of exchange, a store of value, and a unit of account. We shall consider each of these functions in turn.

A medium of exchange. When we use money to pay the rent, to purchase a car, to pay for books, or to buy a ticket to the movies, it is functioning as a medium of exchange. When money functions as a medium of exchange, it circulates in the economy, i.e., it passes from hand to hand. The medium-of-exchange function is the main function of money.

A store of value. As a store of value, money allows individuals to store purchasing power. Of course, it is possible to store some goods, but money is the most convenient form in which purchasing power can be stored. As a store of value, money represents a claim on future goods and services. A good example of money functioning as a store of value is savings.

A unit of account. It is convenient to be able to express values of commodities in terms of a single unit. When money is used as a common denominator in which all other values are expressed, it is functioning as a unit of account. Thus when we say that the price of a text book is $10, that is money functioning as a unit of account. Money serves as a unit of account also when, for example, we keep a daily or weekly budget.

DESIRABLE CHARACTERISTICS OF MONEY

For money to perform its three functions well, it must have certain characteristics. These characteristics may be discussed under the headings of general acceptability, divisibility, durability, cognizability, stability of value, and portability.

General acceptability. The most important characteristic of money is that it must be acceptable. If the item designated to be money ceases to be readily acceptable, it will not be able to perform its most important function – the medium-of-exchange function. If people will not accept a certain item as payment for goods and services, they may resort to barter.

Divisibility. Some transactions require a large amount of money while others require only small amounts. To facilitate small purchases, money must be divisible, i.e., it must be capable of being broken down into small denominations. It is important also that money keeps its value after it has been broken down into smaller denominations. Thus if we change a $20 bill into four $5 bills or ten $2 bills, there should be no loss of value.

Durability. If money is to serve as a store of value, then the item which serves as money should be durable. It is partly because of the durability of gold and silver that those metals have served so well as money. A perishable item would never perform the store of value function of money very well.

Cognizability. No item will be generally acceptable in exchange for goods and services unless it can easily be recognized. It should not be easy to confuse the item which serves as money with some other item. If identification is difficult, traders will be hesitant to part with their goods and services in exchange for something which might be a fake.

Stability of value.   Any item which is used to perform
the store of value function of money
must have a stable value. Money whose value is subject to wide
fluctuations will not serve well as a store of value because it would be
impossible to determine the volume of goods that stored up money
will be able to buy. In an inflation, money loses its value. This
explains why in an inflation, people tend to hold their wealth in real
assets rather than in the form of money.

Portability.   Transactions are not confined to any
one place. People need to carry
around money with them from place to place. A cumbersome item
would make this very inconvenient. People should be able to carry
around a very large sum of money as easily as they carry around a
small sum.

FIAT CURRENCY AND LEGAL TENDER MONEY

Paper currency is a widely used form of money. If the paper money is
backed by gold, it can be "converted" into gold by presenting it to the
bank which issues it, and demanding gold instead. A country which
operates on this system is said to be on the *gold standard*. If the
country's currency is not convertible into gold or any other precious
metal, it is said to be *fiat* money. A fiat is a decree or an order. Fiat
currency serves as money not because of its intrinsic value or because
it is convertible into something valuable, but because people are
willing to accept it in exchange for goods and services, and because
the government declares it to be *legal tender*. The declaration that
paper money is legal tender means that if a debtor pays a creditor
with money declared to be legal tender, the creditor is obliged by law
to accept payment. If he refuses to accept payment, the debt is legally
considered to be discharged.

THE MONEY SUPPLY

The money supply consists of currency (notes and coins), and *demand
deposits*. Demand deposits are chequing accounts. The depositor earns
no interest on demand deposits, but he has the convenience of transferring funds by writing cheques on his account. *Notice deposits* (savings accounts) are sometimes included in the money supply. Notice
deposits can easily be converted into currency or demand deposits.
Interest is earned on notice deposits, but notice deposits are not
transferable by cheques. In Canada, depositors can earn interest on
funds deposited in what is known as a chequable savings account. The

interest is lower than that paid on notice deposit accounts, but the depositor has the convenience of writing cheques on these accounts.

If the money supply is defined as consisting only of currency outside chartered banks and demand deposits, economists refer to this definition as the narrow definition of money and denote it by the symbol M_1. If the definition is broadened to include notice deposits, then economists refer to this broad definition of money as M_2.

The concept of near-money.

When a consumer receives his income, he may decide to keep a part of it for a while before passing it on in exchange for goods and services. This amount may be kept in the form of a savings account, or in the form of some other asset. These assets will not now function as a medium of exchange, but will serve as a temporary store of value to bridge the gap between the time when income is received and the time when expenditure is made. Obviously, assets which can easily be converted into the medium of exchange will serve this function most satisfactorily. Such assets are referred to as *near-money*. We have seen that notice deposits are a good example of near-money, although it is debatable whether they should be classified as near-money or as money. Another example of near money would be short-term government bonds.

Credit versus money.

There is some misunderstanding regarding the popular credit cards. In some quarters, these items which facilitate credit have been termed *plastic money*. The question is, should Master Charge or Chargex, for example, be considered as money? True, these widely used credit cards allow their holders to obtain goods and services without the use of currency or demand deposits. But there is a great difference between offering a credit card as payment and offering currency or demand deposits. When currency or demand deposit is used, the debt is discharged and the transaction is completed. However, with a credit card, the transaction is not completed. The offer of a credit card simply identifies the debtor to whom credit has been extended. The final settlement will have to be made with currency or demand deposit at some future date. Therefore, no matter what they may be called, credit cards should not be confused with money.

THE QUANTITY THEORY OF MONEY

It has been observed for a very long time that there is a link between the quantity of money and the general price level. An American economist named Irving Fisher formulated the relationship between the money supply and the price level into the *Quantity Theory of Money*. Let us take a look at this theory.

let M = the quantity of money

$\quad V$ = the income velocity of circulation of money, i.e., the number of times per year, on an average, that a dollar changes hands.

$\quad P$ = the general price level

$\quad T$ = the physical output of the economy.

If we take the product of M and V, we obtain total expenditure. For example, if on the average, each dollar is spent four times per year, then total expenditure from \$250 will be \$1,000. If we take the product of P and T, we obtain the value of total output. Now the value of total output must be equal to total expenditure on that output. Thus what we have is an identity which can be written as

$$MV \equiv PT \text{ (the Fisher equation of exchange).}$$

As it stands, this identity says nothing but that the total value of goods bought equals the total value of goods sold. But by making certain assumptions, the identity can be transformed into a hypothesis. The quantity theorists made two basic assumptions: (1) that the income velocity of circulation of money (V) was constant, and (2) that physical output (T) was always at its full-employment level. Thus we have

$$MV = PT$$

By dividing by V we obtain

$$M = \frac{PT}{V}$$

Since T is always at its full-employment level, and since V is constant, then $\dfrac{T}{V}$ is constant.

Let $k = \dfrac{T}{V}$ then the above equation can be written as

$$M = kP$$

This tells us that if the money supply doubles, the price level will double; and if the money supply falls by ten percent, the price level will fall by ten percent. This simple version of the quantity theory says simply that any change in the money supply will cause a proportional change in the general level of prices.

A modern and more sophisticated version of the quantity theory of money has been formulated. Particularly, it is no longer generally held that the velocity of circulation is constant. Instead, modern quantity theorists believe that although V changes from year to year, the changes are relatively slow and are predictable. Emphasis has shifted to the demand for money, and modern quantity theorists now link changes in the money supply to changes in nominal (money) national income.

THE KEYNESIAN THEORY OF MONEY

According to the views of the early quantity theorists, the demand for money was for transaction purposes only, and this depended on the level of income. In the Keynesian approach, there are three motives for holding money: the transactions motive, the precautionary motive, and the speculative motive.

The transactions motive.   Households and firms hold money balances for transactions because the receipt of income and expenditure outlays do not coincide. Income may be received once or twice per month while expenditures are made much more frequently. There will therefore be a need to hold some cash balances so that transactions can be made between one income payment date and the next. Keynes postulated that the transactions demand for money was a function of the level of income. The higher the level of income, the greater the amount of money held for transaction purposes. Figure 10-1 illustrates this relationship.

FIG. 10-1

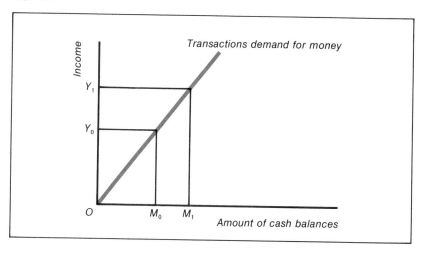

Income is plotted on the vertical axis and the amount of money held for transactions is plotted on the horizontal axis. At a level of income of Y_0, the amount of money held for transaction purposes is M_0. When income increases to Y_1, the amount of money balances held for transaction purposes increases to M_1.

The precautionary motive.   In addition to holding a certain amount of money balances for transactions, people may hold some extra cash balances to safeguard themselves against unforeseen contingencies—just in case something happens. Keynes referred to this motive for holding money balances as the *precautionary motive*. The demand for money for precautionary purposes, according to Keynes, depends on the level of income in much the same way as the transactions demand.

The speculative motive.   Keynes noted that people may hold money balances for speculative purposes. To see what is involved, let us assume that people can hold financial assets in only two forms: money balances which earn no interest, and bonds which earn interest. It is helpful at this point to introduce the relationship between the price of bonds and the rate of interest. A simple arithmetic example will suffice. The yield on a bond is fixed. Suppose a bond purchased for $100 yields $5 annually. The purchaser could consider that he earns five percent interest. Now suppose the price of the bond increases to $125. The yield of $5 annually now represents only four percent interest. This simple arithmetic example illustrates the important point that there is an inverse relation between the price of bonds and the interest rate. To say that the rate of interest rises is equivalent to saying that bond prices fall.

If bond prices are low (interest rates are high) and people expect them to rise (interest rates to fall), they will buy bonds now and sell them in the future when the price rises, thus making a profit. By buying bonds now, people would be reducing their money balances. Thus, the higher the rate of interest, the smaller the quantity of money balances that will be held. If bond prices are high now (the rate of interest is low) and people expect them to fall (the rate of interest to rise) in the future, they will convert their bonds into cash before the price actually falls, i.e., they will increase their money balances. The lower the rate of interest, the greater will be the amount of money balances that people will wish to hold. Figure 10-2 illustrates this inverse relation between the rate of interest and the amount of money balances.

At a rate of interest of r_o, the amount of money held is M_1. When the rate rises to r_1, the amount of money held falls to M_o. The desire to hold assets in the form of money balances rather than in the form of bonds is called *liquidity preference*, and the curve shown in the above diagram is a liquidity preference curve.

DETERMINATION OF THE RATE OF INTEREST

In this section, we shall examine two theories of the determination of the rate of interest: the Classical loanable funds theory, and the Keynesian liquidity preference theory. The term "Classical Econo-

FIG. 10-2

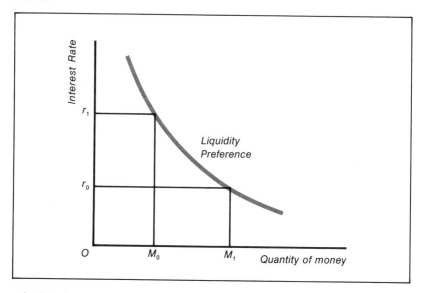

mists" refers to the 19th Century and early 20th Century economists. The era of the Classical economists can be dated from the time of David Ricardo (1772-1823) right up to the late 1920s or early 1930s.

The classical loanable funds theory. According to this theory, the rate of interest was determined by the demand for investment funds and by the supply of savings. Figure 10-3 illustrates the determination of the rate of interest.

The demand for investment funds comes from the firms. The higher the rate of interest, the less funds the firms will wish to borrow. This gives the downward sloping demand curve DD shown in the diagram. The supply of investment funds comes from savings. The lower the rate of interest, the lower will be the level of saving; and the higher the rate of interest, the higher will be the level of saving. This gives the upward sloping supply curve SS shown in the diagram. The intersection of the demand and supply curves at E determines the equilibrium rate of interest $\bar{r}$.

The liquidity preference theory. The liquidity preference theory follows an entirely different approach from that of the Classical theory. The demand for money in this Keynesian liquidity preference approach, is the demand for money to hold in cash balances. We have seen in a previous section that this amount varies inversely with the rate of interest. The liquidity preference schedule is a demand for money schedule. In Figure 10-4 the demand curve DD shows that a greater

FIG. 10-3

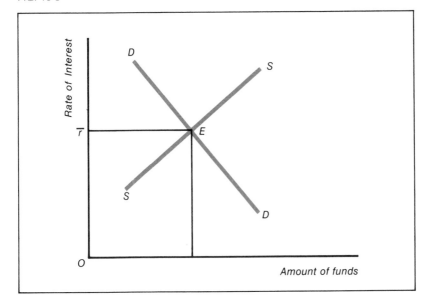

FIG. 10-4

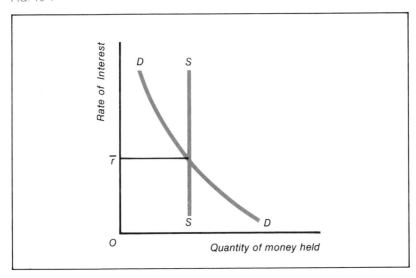

quantity of money is held at lower rates of interest. The supply of money *SS* is fixed by the banking system and is therefore represented by a vertical line. The intersection of this supply curve with the demand curve determines the equilibrium rate of interest $\bar{r}$. We will return to the liquidity preference theory when we study monetary policy in a later chapter.

CHAPTER 11
COMMERCIAL BANKING

The banking system consists of the central bank and a number of commercial banks. In this chapter we will focus attention on the operation of commercial banks. A commercial bank is a privately owned financial institution. Commercial banking is a business, and like any other business, a commercial bank's main objective is to earn profits for its shareholders. We shall see how commercial banks' activities can and do affect the money supply. Commercial banks are often called *chartered banks* because they operate under government charter. In Canada, the charter (i.e., the authority to operate) is granted by the federal government. In the United States, some banks are chartered by the federal government while others are chartered by state governments. In Canada, there are about twelve commercial banks, each with hundreds of branches scattered all over the country. This system is referred to as a *branch banking system*. In the United States, the system consists of a large number of independent banks. This system is referred to as a *unit banking system*. An exception to this is the state of California where branch banking has existed for a long time.

Banking services. Commercial banks' earnings are derived from a number of services which they provide. The most important of these services is the establishment of convenient demand deposit accounts. The opportunity of transferring funds by writing cheques eliminates the need to carry around huge sums of cash. Most transactions involving huge sums of money are made by cheques. A second important service rendered by commercial banks is that of extending loans. Households and firms often need to borrow funds for one reason or another. Commercial banks are a good source for such funds. By purchasing government bonds, commercial banks extend loans to the government. There are other sources from which loans can be obtained but the rate of interest charged is usually higher than that charged by the commercial banks. A third service provided by commercial banks is the establishment of savings accounts. Individuals may deposit funds in savings accounts and earn a return on their savings. Finally, commercial banks offer a number of other services including a wide range of financial advice, the convenience of bill payment (a variety of bills can be paid at commercial banks), the provision of the means whereby the exchange of foreign currency can take place, and the safe keeping of valuables and important documents. Commercial banks derive more than 80 percent of their earnings from the interest charged on loans and from other investment. Less than 20 percent is derived from fees charged for services.

Clearing of cheques.   Let us assume that Mr. Adams and Mr. Burns keep their accounts at the same bank A. If Mr. Adams writes a cheque to Mr. Burns for $500, Mr. Burns takes the cheque to bank A and either cashes it or deposits it in his account. If he cashes it, the bank pays him $500 and reduces Mr. Adams' account by $500. But suppose Mr. Adams keeps his account at bank A and Mr. Burns keeps his at bank B. The cheque for $500 is presented to bank B by Mr. Burns. Bank B increases Mr. Burns' account by $500 and has a cheque which indicates a claim on bank A for $500. A customer who keeps his account in bank B may write a cheque to someone who keeps his account in bank A. Let us assume that the amount of the cheque is $400. Bank B now owes bank A $400. The account between banks A and B can be settled by a payment of $100 from bank A to bank B.

A number of such transactions are made each day and the banks clear their cheques through a *clearing house system*. At the end of each day, the cheques written by customers of the various banks are added up and the indebtedness of one bank to another is thus determined. Now each commercial bank in Canada has a deposit at the Bank of Canada which is the central bank. If it is determined by the clearing house system that bank A has to make a net payment of $5,000 to bank B at the end of a day's operation, then the central bank simply increases bank B's deposit by $5,000 and reduces bank A's deposit by $5,000, and the account is settled.

MONEY CREATION BY THE BANKING SYSTEM

By pursuing their objective of profit maximization, commercial banks engage in activities which lead to the creation of deposits as a by-product of their profit-seeking activities. To simplify the analysis of money creation by commercial banks, we make the following assumptions.

1. There is a single bank with a number of branches. This is often referred to as a monopoly bank.
2. The bank is obliged by law to keep ten percent of its deposits in the form of cash. The percentage of deposits held as cash reserves is called the *reserve ratio* or the *legal reserve requirement*.

3. Any additional funds obtained by any member of the community are held in the form of demand deposits. There is therefore no *currency drain* from the system.
4. Loans are the only investments the bank makes.
5. The bank wants to be *fully loaned up*. This means that the bank will be willing to lend out any *excess reserves* it may acquire. Excess reserves are reserves held over and above the minimum legal reserve requirement.
6. The bank has no trouble finding customers who want to borrow.

T-accounts will be helpful in explaining the process of money creation. A T-account shows the changes in the bank's balance sheet as a result of some specific transaction. In order to understand how entries are made in the T-account, we must understand the terms *asset* and *liability*. An *asset* is anything that is owned by an institution. A *liability*, on the other hand, represents an institution's indebtedness to someone else. Deposits are obviously a liability of the bank since the bank owes its depositors the amounts deposited.

Suppose depositor A deposits $100 in his demand deposit account. This deposit increases the bank's deposit liabilities by $100 and its assets (in the form of currency) by an equivalent amount. This deposit transaction will appear as follows on the bank's T-account.

Assets		Liabilities	
Reserves (currency)	$100	Deposits	$100

The bank is legally bound to keep ten percent of its deposits as required reserve. The bank therefore has $90 excess reserves which it can lend out. If a customer (call him Mr. B) borrows this $90, the bank deposits it in his account and he is able to write cheques on this account up to a value of $90. This loan transaction now appears on the bank's T-account as follows:

Assets		Liabilities	
Reserves (currency)	$100	Deposits:	
Loans	90	Mr. A	$100
		Mr. B	90
	$100		$100

This process of extending a loan by increasing a customer's demand deposit account is known as *monetizing a loan*. The original deposit of

$100 is called an *initial* or *primary deposit*. The deposit which results from the loan is known as a *secondary* or *derivative* deposit. Mr. A now has $100 in his account, and Mr. B has $90 in his account, making a total of $190. We started with only $100. Where did the additional $90 come from? The bank created it. The bank is obliged to keep ten percent of Mr. B's deposit as cash reserves. It can therefore lend out the remaining $81. By extending a loan of $81, the bank will again create a new deposit. The process continues until excess reserves have been exhausted. At this point, the balance sheet will appear as follows:

Assets		Liabilities	
Reserves (currency)	$100	Deposits:	
Loans	900	Mr. A	$100
		Mr. B	90
		Mr. C	81
		.	.
		.	.
		.	.
	$1,000		$1,000

This step-by-step process is illustrated in the following table.

Steps	Deposits ($)	Reserve Requirement ($)	Loans ($)
1	100	10	90
2	90	9	81
3	81	8.10	72.90
4	72.90	7.29	65.61
5	64.61	6.56	59.05
:	:	:	:
:	:	:	:
:	:	:	:
.	.	.	.
Sum	1,000	100	900

If the reserve ratio is ten percent, then total deposits will be ten times the initial deposit. In general, if the reserve ratio is R, the multiple by which the initial deposit must be multiplied up to give the total deposits is $\frac{1}{R}$. The following formula will be found to be quite useful.

$$D = d \cdot \frac{1}{R}$$

where D = total deposits
d = initial deposits
R = reserve ratio

The number $\frac{1}{R}$ is usually referred to as the *bank multiplier* or the *money multiplier*. Note that the amount of money created by the bank is total deposits minus the initial deposit. This should be obvious since the bank did not create the initial deposit. Since the bank's reserves enable it to increase deposits, the reserves are sometimes called *high-powered money*.

An example. Calculate the amount of money that a bank can create out of a deposit of $500 given a reserve ratio of 20 percent. In this example, d = $500 and R = 1/5. Applying the formula

$$D = d . \frac{1}{R}$$, we obtain

$$D = 500 \ \frac{1}{\frac{1}{5}} = (500 \times 5) = 2,500.$$

Total deposits will amount to $2,500. But the initial deposit is $500, therefore the amount that the bank will be able to create is $(2500 − 500) = $2,000.

Throughout the analysis, we have assumed that there is only one bank. The process of money creation in a multibank system is more complicated than in the single bank system which we have examined, but the result is the same. Also, we have considered only the case of money creation. If money is withdrawn from an account, the total money supply will fall by several times the amount withdrawn–the multiplier works in reverse also. The student is advised to work through the analysis of money destruction.

A MOVEMENT TOWARDS REALISM

In the preceding analysis of money creation, we assumed that there was no currency drain, that the bank did not keep any excess reserves, and that loans were the only investment the bank made. Under these assumptions, the maximum amount by which the bank could increase its deposits was $\frac{1}{R}$ times the amount of new money it received. In the real world, it is unlikely that people will want to hold all the extra money they receive in the form of deposits. They will most likely want to hold some cash. The desire to hold cash reduces the banks' ability to create money. If there is a currency drain to the public, the money multiplier will be smaller than if there is no currency drain.

The assumption that banks lend out all their excess reserves has to be modified. For one reason or another, banks may not wish to lend out all their excess reserves, and even if they wanted to, they may not succeed because households and firms may be unwilling to borrow. This is another factor which limits the amount of money that the banks can create. It must be recognized also that loans are not the only type of investment that banks make. They can invest in many different kinds of assets. If, however, instead of extending loans to their customers, the banks buy bonds, the money creating process remains unchanged. The bonds would be paid for by cheques drawn on the banks and these cheques would be deposited on the banks by the bond sellers.

CHAPTER 12

CENTRAL BANKING AND MONETARY POLICY

Changes in the money supply can affect income, employment and prices. In this chapter, we shall look at the functions of the central bank and examine the methods that it uses to control the money supply. In England, the central bank is the Bank of England. Here in Canada, it is the Bank of Canada, and in the United States, it is called the Federal Reserve System.

FUNCTIONS OF A CENTRAL BANK

A central bank performs four main functions. These are:

(1) *To distribute currency.* The central bank is responsible for seeing that the country has an adequate supply of currency. In performing this function, the central bank must ensure that its issue of new bank notes is not too great. Irresponsible increases in currency can have serious adverse effects on the economy.

(2) *To act as banker to the government.* The government keeps its chequing account with the central bank just as you and I keep our accounts at a commercial bank. In our discussion of fiscal policy, we noted that the government often borrows funds to finance its programmes. Some of these loans come from the central bank. The central bank makes loans to the government by buying government securities and paying for them by increasing the government's deposit account by the value of the securities.

(3) *To act as banker to the commercial banks.* The cash reserves of the commercial banks are held in the form of deposits at the central bank and currency in their vaults. If the commercial banks need to borrow money, they borrow from the central bank, and we have already seen that the central bank plays an important role in the cheque clearing operations of commercial banks. The function of lending money to the commercial banks when they need it is often referred to as the *lender of last resort* function.

(4) *To conduct the country's monetary policy.* The central bank is charged with the responsibility of conducting the government's monetary policy. Monetary policy works through changes in the money supply and the interest rate. Below, we examine the instruments which the central bank uses to conduct monetary policy.

MONETARY POLICY

Monetary policy can be defined as changes in the money supply and the rate of interest designed to influence the economy. The primary objectives of monetary policy are to maintain a high level of employment and relative price stability. We shall see how the central bank uses monetary policy to reduce inflation and to stimulate the economy.

The instruments of monetary policy. The central bank has four main tools which it can use to control the money supply and interest rates. They are open-market operations, changes in the bank rate, changes in the reserve ratio, and moral suasion.

Open-market operations. Open-market operations may be defined as the buying and selling of government securities by the central bank on the open market. If the central bank wants to increase the money supply, it can buy securities on the open market. If it buys securities from commercial banks, it pays for them by increasing the deposit accounts of the commercial banks at the central bank. These new reserves now enable the commercial banks to expand loans and thus increase the money supply. If the central bank buys securities from the public, it pays for them by offering cheques drawn on the central bank. These cheques are deposited in commercial banks which present them to the central bank for payment. The central bank increases the deposits of the commercial banks at the central bank, and with this new deposit, the multiple expansion process is possible.

If the central bank sells securities to the public on the open market, they are paid for by cheques drawn on commercial banks. The central bank presents the cheques to the commercial banks, and payment is made to the central bank by a reduction in the commercial banks' deposits with the central bank. If the central bank sells securities to the commercial banks, the securities will be paid for by reducing the commercial banks' deposits at the central bank. In either case, the result is a decrease in the money supply.

The open-market operations that we have described above serve as the most important weapon available to the central bank to vary the money supply. Open-market operations are an extremely effective means of changing the reserves of the commercial banks.

Changes in the bank rate. The *bank rate* is the rate of interest which commercial banks have to pay when they borrow from the central bank. If the central bank wants to increase the money supply, it can lower the bank rate to encourage borrowing by the commercial banks. If the central bank wants to decrease the money supply, it can raise the bank rate and thus discourage borrowing. Changes in the bank rate are not likely to be very effective as a means of controlling the money supply because borrowing from the central bank is limited. This instrument is rather passive and serves more as a signal of the policy the central bank is pursuing.

Changes in the reserve ratio.

Changes in the reserve requirement can be used as a powerful weapon to control the money supply. It is evident by looking at the multiplier $\frac{1}{R}$ that changes in R affect the value of the multiplier. If the central bank changes the reserve ratio from 10 to 20 percent, the commercial banks will have to keep a larger amount of cash reserves, thus their ability to increase loans and create new deposits will be reduced. On the other hand, a reduction in the reserve ratio will increase the banks' ability to extend loans and make possible a larger increase in new deposits. At present in Canada, the central bank does not use this tool to conduct monetary policy. The reserve ratio for demand deposits and notice deposits have been established at 12 and 4 percent respectively. The Bank of Canada has the power to impose a minimum secondary reserve requirement on commercial banks. *Secondary reserves* may be defined as day-to-day loans to investment dealers, treasury bills, and cash in excess of the legal reserve requirement. The ratio of secondary reserves to deposits is termed the *secondary reserve ratio*. The Bank of Canada may vary this ratio between zero and 12 percent, but may not increase it by more than one percentage point per month.

Moral suasion.

Moral suasion may be defined as an appeal from the central bank to the commercial banks to cooperate with the monetary policy being pursued by the central bank. For example, if the central bank wants to pursue a "tight money" policy (i.e., a reduction in the money supply to restrict total spending), it can make its intention known and enlist the support of the commercial banks to restrict their loan activities. Moral suasion can easily be used in Canada because the relatively small number of commercial banks makes communication between the central bank and the commercial banks relatively easy.

THE EFFECTS OF MONETARY POLICY

Let us see how changes in the money supply may affect aggregate

FIG. 12-1A, 12-1B

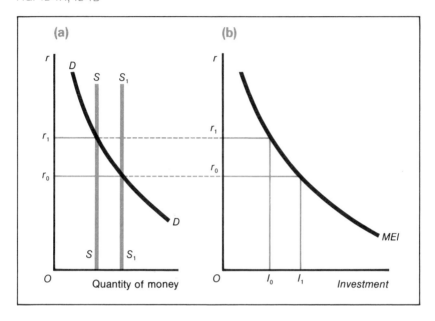

demand. In Chapter 10 we showed that the rate of interest was determined by the intersection of the demand curve for money and the supply curve for money. In Figure 12-1A, an increase in the supply of money from SS to S_1S_1 causes the rate of interest to fall from r_1 to r_0. The fall in the rate of interest will cause an increase in investment as can be seen from Figure 12-1B. The fall in the rate of interest from r_1 to r_0 leads to an increase in investment from I_0 to I_1. There may also be an increase in consumption resulting from the reduction in the rate of interest (see Chapter 7). The increase in investment will set off a chain reaction in spending, and total income will increase to several times the increase in investment, depending on the multiplier.

Monetary policy and unemployment.

We have seen how a government may use fiscal policy to reduce the level of unemployment in the country. In this section, we shall see how the central bank may use monetary policy to achieve its objective of a high level of employment. Figure 12-2 shows a situation where the economy has settled down to a less than full-employment equilibrium.

The figure is similar to the one used in discussing fiscal policy. There is a deflationary gap—aggregate demand is inadequte to produce full employment. The appropriate monetary policy in this case is an expansionary monetary policy. An increase in the money supply

FIG. 12-2

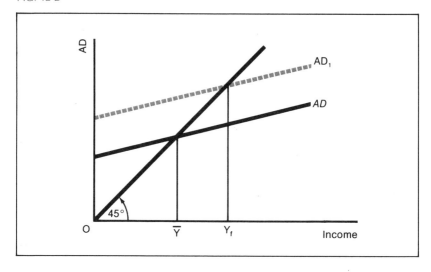

will lower the rate of interest which will cause an increase in investment and consumption. The aggregate demand function will increase from AD to AD_1 and the unemployment will be eliminated—equilibrium will be at the full-employment (Y_f) level. The appropriate monetary policy in an inflationary situation is a reduction in the money supply. The analysis in this case is left as an exercise for the student to work through.

The effectiveness of monetary policy.

How effective is monetary policy in achieving the objective of full employment? The answer to this question depends on the effect of changes in the money supply on the rate of interest and on the effect of changes in the rate of interest on investment. If the increase in the money supply reduces the rate of interest significantly, and if the reduction in the rate of interest causes a large increase in investment, then monetary policy will be an effective means of stimulating the economy.

In Figure 12-3A below, an increase in the money supply from SS to S_1S_1 is very effective in lowering the rate of interest from r_1 to r_0. Figure 12-3B shows that a fall in the rate of interest from r_1 to r_0 is very effective in increasing the level of investment. This implies that monetary policy will be an effective means of increasing aggregate demand if the demand for money schedule is inelastic (steep) and if the MEI schedule is elastic (flat).

It is possible to have a situation in which increases in the money supply have little or no effect on the rate of interest. Such a situation

FIG. 12-3A, 12-3B

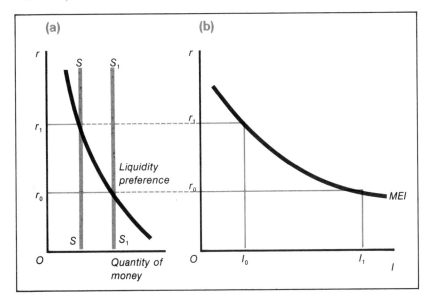

FIG. 12-4

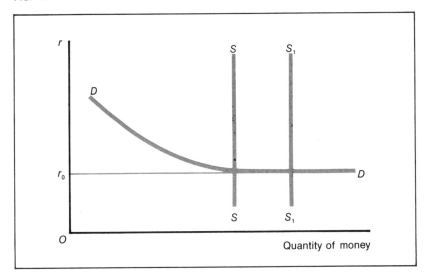

is illustrated in Figure 12-4. The demand for money schedule becomes flat at a rate of interest of r_0. Further increases in the money supply have no effect in lowering the rate of interest, and monetary policy will be ineffective. This situation is referred to as the *liquidity trap*. In this case, fiscal policy will have to be invoked in order to stimulate aggregate demand.

Monetary policy may be effective in lowering the rate of interest and still fail to stimulate the economy. Even if the rate of interest falls as a result of an increase in the money supply, the lower rate of interest may have little or no effect in stimulating investment. This could happen if businessmen expect a significant long term decrease in demand. This possibility is illustrated in Figures 12-5A and 12-5B.

FIG. 12-5A, 12-5B

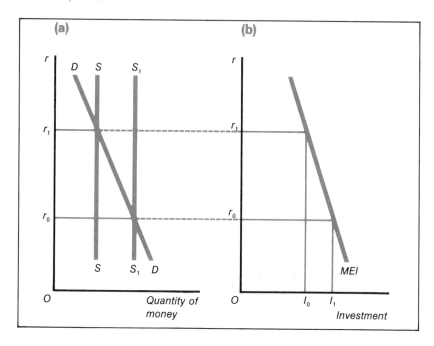

Figure 12-5A shows that monetary policy is very effective in lowering the rate of interest. In Figure 12-5B however, the *MEI* schedule is very steep. The significant fall in the rate of interest does not produce a significant rise in the level of investment. In other words, investment is insensitive to changes in the rate of interest, hence monetary policy may not be very effective.

POST-KEYNESIANS AND MONETARISTS

We have shown that changes in the money supply can affect aggregate demand through the interest rate, but that there are other factors which can also influence aggregate demand. We have also shown that in certain circumstances, monetary policy may not be effective. These conclusions are in the Keynesian tradition and may be termed *post-*

Keynesian or *neo-Keynesian*. A group of economists known as *monetarists* believe that changes in aggregate demand are due mainly to changes in the money supply. Although they usually follow a different type of analysis from the one presented above, their position seems to be that increases in the money supply will produce large reductions in the rate of interest which in turn will produce large increases in the level of investment. They believe also that in order to avoid fluctuations in the economy, the central bank should increase the money supply at a steady rate from year to year instead of attempting to "fine tune" the economy.

In the monetarists' view, fiscal policy as a means of stimulating the economy will not be very effective if it is not accompanied by an increase in the money supply. An increase in government spending, for example, will increase income. As income increases, there will be an increase in the demand for money. This will cause the rate of interest to rise. This rise in the rate of interest will tend to discourage investment and thus cancel out the stimulating effect of the increase in government spending. Therefore to prevent the rate of interest from rising, the money supply must be increased.

It is probably true to say that the neo-Keynesians and the monetarists are now much closer than they were a few years ago. There are however, major areas of disagreement and the debate continues. A number of studies have been undertaken with a view to determining whether the monetarists or the neo-Keynesians are right, but until more conclusive studies have been undertaken, the controversy is likely to continue.

CHAPTER 13

UNEMPLOYMENT AND INFLATION

UNEMPLOYMENT

Labour is the most important factor of production, therefore unemployment represents a waste of the economy's most valuable resource. Unemployment and inflation are the two most serious economic problems facing the country today. Unemployment may be defined as a situation in which people who are willing to work at the existing wage rate are unable to find jobs. This definition of the unemployed excludes all those individuals who are not seeking employment. Such persons are said to be "voluntarily" unemployed, and should be distinguished from the "involuntary" unemployment defined above. In our study of unemployment, we shall be concerned only with involuntary unemployment.

The *labour force* consists of those individuals who are willing to work at the existing wage rate (i.e., the employed and the involuntarily unemployed). People who are not working and are unwilling to work are not a part of the labour force. The unemployment situation is usually reported as a percentage—*the unemployment rate*—which measures the proportion of the labour force that is unemployed. Given a labour force of 10,500,000 and an unemployment figure of 600,000, the unemployment rate is $(\frac{600,000}{10,500,000} \times 100) = 5.7$ percent , approximately. The unemployment rate for Canada from 1960 to 1976 is given in the first column of Table 13-1.

Types of unemployment. A number of different types of unemployment can be identified according to the factors causing the unemployment. We list below some of the major types of unemployment.

Frictional unemployment. At any point in time, there will be some people who are in between jobs. People sometimes quit their jobs, some are dismissed, and some may be just entering the labour force (e.g., new graduates). Jobs may be available for these people but they will be temporarily unemployed. This type of unemployment is called *frictional unemployment*. Full employment is said to exist if the only type of unemployment the economy is experiencing is frictional unemployment.

Structural unemployment. A number of factors may cause some industries to expand and others to contract. For example, there may be a long term fall in demand for the products of some industries, causing them to contract or to go out of business entirely. Although other industries may be expanding, the unemployed may not be able to find employment in these expanding industries for reasons such as inappropriate skills and unwillingness on the part of the unemployed to relocate. This type of unemployment is called *structural unemployment* since it is related to changes in the structure of the economy.

Table 13-1. Unemployment Rate and Consumer Price Index, Canada 1960-76

Year	Unemployment Rate (%)	CPI (1971 = 100)
1960	7.0	76.3
1961	7.1	76.8
1962	5.9	77.8
1963	5.5	79.0
1964	4.7	80.0
1965	3.9	81.6
1966	3.6	84.3
1967	4.1	87.2
1968	4.8	90.8
1969	4.7	94.3
1970	5.9	97.7
1971	6.4	100.0
1972	6.3	104.0
1973	5.6	111.6
1974	5.4	123.9
1975	6.9	137.1
1976	7.1	147.2

Source: Statistics Canada, The Labour Force, and Canada Year Book.

Cyclical unemployment. Unemployment associated with business fluctuations is called *cyclical unemployment*. Cyclical unemployment is the result of a deficiency of aggregate demand. If total expenditure declines, firms reduce production and therefore do not hire as many workers. We have already looked at this type of unemployment when we studied fiscal policy and monetary policy.

Seasonal Unemployment.   Certain types of activities are performed only at certain times in the year. For example, construction slows down during the winter months, activities related to winter sports decline in the summer months, and agricultural activities are significantly reduced in the winter months. This type of unemployment which is related to seasonal changes is termed *seasonal unemployment*.

The costs of   It is obvious that an unemployed person suffers a loss of income. His family may be forced to make sacrifices in terms of reduced consumption. But unemployment represents a real loss to the economy. It has been argued that the establishment of unemployment insurance reduces the problem of unemployment. Unemployment compensation certainly reduces the difficulties that the unemployed have to face. But output lost by unemployment can never be regained. The economic cost of unemployment can be measured in terms of lost output or in terms of lost income. *Potential GNP* is that output which the economy would be able to produce with full employment. Potential *GNP* is sometimes called full-employment output. *Actual output* is the output actually produced and measured by the techniques discussed in Chapter 5. The difference between potential *GNP* and actual *GNP* is a measure of the output lost because of unemployment. The alternative method of estimating the cost of unemployment involves multiplying the number of unemployed persons by the average annual wage. The resulting figure will be an estimate of the loss in national income due to unemployment.

We have thus far concentrated only on the economic aspects of the cost of unemployment. But the social aspect of the cost of unemployment may be even more serious than the economic aspect. Unemployment can cause serious social problems. People may become discouraged and frustrated when they are unable to find employment, and dissatisfaction may cause them to resort to violence, theft, destruction of property and a number of other undesirable activities. Family happiness may be permanently destroyed and the self-esteem of the unemployed may be lost forever. Statistics on unemployment cannot adequately measure these costs, but they are real and often greater than the measurable economic aspects of the cost of unemployment.

INFLATION

Price stability was cited as one of the objectives of macro-economic policy. Canada, along with many other countries, has experienced relatively high rates of inflation in recent years. Indeed, inflation is seen today as one of the nation's most serious economic problems. Inflation may be defined as a persistent rise in the price level. In an inflation, not all prices will be rising; some prices may even be falling, but the average price level will rise since most prices will be rising.

The rate of inflation measures the annual percentage increase in the price level. If the rate of increase is very low, say two or three percent annually, the term *creeping inflation* is used. A faster rate of inflation, say 15 percent, is referred to as *galloping inflation*; and a much more rapid increase, say 25 to 30 percent, is termed *hyper-inflation*. In recent times, we have witnessed high rates of inflation simultaneously with high unemployment. This phenomenon has been christened *stagflation*. The *consumer price index* (*CPI*) which shows the increase in the average price level of consumer goods and services is shown in the second column of Table 13-1.

The effects of inflation.   Whenever there is inflation, some groups will benefit while others will lose. Those whose incomes increase at a faster rate than the increase in the price level will gain. The gainers include debtors who pay back a smaller amount in real terms during an inflation, and people who sell products whose prices rise faster than production costs. On the other hand some people suffer a loss of income because of inflation. These people include creditors and people such as pensioners who are on fixed incomes. Such people suffer a real loss of purchasing power during an inflation. These remarks apply largely where the inflation is not anticipated. If the inflation is anticipated, people can protect themselves against it. Creditors can charge higher rates, households can convert their savings into real assets, and workers can negotiate for contracts which include automatic increases in wages to compensate for inflation.

An economy's productive capacity is built up by its investment. But investment is impossible without saving. Inflation may discourage saving since a given sum of money saved up is worth less in the future if there is inflation. The reduction in saving means a reduction in investment and hence a lower level of output. Contrary to this view, it has been argued that a mild inflation may serve as a stimulus to the economy. We have suggested that inflation tends to discourage saving and encourage spending. This increase in spending may have an expansionary effect on output and employment. Some economists express the view that during an inflation, product prices rise at a faster rate than factor prices, hence profits increase during an inflation. This increase in profits may stimulate investment which in turn will cause output and employment to increase.

TYPES OF INFLATION

There are two main types of inflation: *demand-pull* inflation and *cost-push* inflation.

Demand-pull inflation. Once an economy has reached its full employment level of output, further increases in the supply of goods and services are not possible in the short run. Thus, if total spending continues to increase after full employment has been reached, prices will tend to rise. Since demand-pull inflation results from an excess of total demand over full-employment output, it has been termed *excess demand* inflation. The phenomenon of an inflationary gap which we have discussed in previous sections is demand-pull inflation. Demand-pull inflation has been typically blamed on excessive increases in the money supply and excessive increases in government spending.

Cost-push inflation. If the cost of production rises because of an increase in factor prices (wages, for example), prices will be pushed up. Higher product prices leads to demands for higher wages to protect the workers' purchasing power. This in turn leads to higher prices, so that a wage-price spiral is set in motion. When inflation exists in the absence of excess demand, it is of the cost-push variety.

THE TRADE-OFF BETWEEN FULL-EMPLOYMENT AND INFLATION

If the economy is in a situation of stagflation, policies to reduce inflation may increase unemployment, and policies to reduce unemployment may increase inflation. Thus a higher level of employment can be achieved only at the expense of a higher rate of inflation. This inverse relationship between inflation and unemployment can be illustrated in Figure 13-1 by the trade-off curve called the *Phillips curve*, named after the British economist A. W. Phillips.

In fact, the relationship studied by Phillips was one between the percentage change in the wage rate and the rate of unemployment, and not a relation between inflation and unemployment. The diagram shows that price stability (i.e., a zero rate of inflation) can be achieved only at an unemployment rate of five percent and that a two percent unemployment rate cannot be achieved without a six percent rate of inflation. Policy makers are therefore caught in a dilemma. The objec-

FIG. 13-1

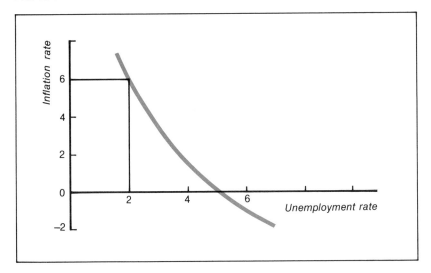

tives of full-employment and price stability seem to be inconsistent, and a decision therefore has to be made regarding the least undesirable combination of unemployment and inflation.

CHAPTER 14

THE BALANCE OF PAYMENTS AND EXCHANGE RATES

The countries of the world today engage in foreign trade, and they keep a record of all transactions made with the rest of the world. Such a record of international transactions is referred to as the *balance of payments*. Recall that $AD = C + I + G + (X - M)$. In this chapter, we study the $(X - M)$ component of aggregate demand. An export item for a country is recorded as a credit in that country's balance of payments, while an import item is recorded as a debit.

The balance of payments accounts contain the *current account* and the *capital account*. The current account contains all sales and purchases of currently produced goods and services. It includes exports and imports of goods (merchandise) and services such as transportation services and tourist services. The capital account contains all transactions not entered in the current account. These include long-term capital flows, short term capital flows, and changes in official reserves. If an American firm establishes a branch in Canada, or if a Canadian company establishes a branch in some foreign country, it is considered direct investment. The purchase of securities with less than a year as the maturity date is an example of short-term capital flows. Finally, countries hold reserves with which international payment can be made. Changes in such reserves are recorded in the capital account. If Canada exports $20 million of goods and services and imports $15 million, then the rest of the world would have to pay $5 million to Canada. The imbalance in the *current* account will be made good in the capital account. The balance of payments always balances (see Table 14-1).

The *balance of trade* is the term used to describe the difference between exports (X) and imports (M). This value is also referred to as *net exports*. If $(X - M)$ is positive, i.e., if there is a surplus of exports over imports, then the country is said to have a favourable balance of trade. But either a surplus or a deficit in the net export account can create problems of unemployment and price instability. If a country's imports exceed its exports, than aggregate demand, $C + I + G + (X - M)$, will be less than if $(X - M)$ were positive. This means that expenditure on domestically produced goods and services will be reduced and this may lead to unemployment. In this case, some action would need to be taken against the deficit. If there is a surplus in the net export account, (i.e., $X - M$), then there is a greater demand for the goods and services produced in the country. If the country is unable to increase its production to the level of aggregate demand, then an inflationary situation will develop and action will be needed to deal with the inflation.

Table 14-1. Canada's Balance of Payments, 1976 ($ million)

	Current receipts (Exports) +	Current payments (Imports) −	Balance
CURRENT ACCOUNT			
Merchandise	38,019	36,887	+ 1,132
Services			
Travel	1,941	3,123	− 1,182
Interest and dividends	796	3,358	− 2,562
Freight and shipping	1,928	2,247	− 319
Other services	2,435	4,374	− 1,939
Total services	7,100	13,102	− 6,002
Total goods & services	45,119	49,989	− 4,870
Transfers			
Inheritances and immigrants' funds	725	174	+ 551
Other transfers	765	775	− 10
Total transfers	1,490	949	+ 541
Total (current account)	46,609	50,938	− 4,329
CAPITAL ACCOUNT			
Long-term capital			
Direct investment			− 950
Portfolio investment			+ 8,679
Other long-term capital			− 181
Total long-term capital			+ 7,548
Short-term capital			
Short-term investments			+ 235
Other short-term capital			− 2,932
Total short-term capital			− 2,697
Total net capital account			+ 4,851
Changes in official reserves			+ 522

Source: Statistics Canada, System of National Accounts, Canadian Statistical Review.

EXCHANGE RATES

If nations engage in trade, there must be some mechanism for converting the currency of one country into the currency of another country. If a Canadian company buys merchandise from a British firm, the

British firm would require to be paid in British currency, because the British firm has to pay its workers in British currency, and its other expenditures are made with British currency. The Canadian company would therefore have to buy British pounds to pay for its merchandise. The amount of Canadian dollars that would have to be offered to be used to purchase British pounds depends on the *exchange rate*. The exchange rate is the rate at which the currency of one country exchanges for the currency of another country. If the Canadian company has to pay $2 for a British pound, then the exchange rate is $2 to £1. The exchange rate is thus the price of foreign currency.

Determination of the exchange rate. Let us see how the exchange rate between dollars and pounds is determined. We assume that no attempt is made to fix the rate of exchange, but that the rate is left to be determined by the market forces of demand and supply. Such an exchange rate is said to be a *flexible* or *freely fluctuating* exchange rate. In Figure 14-1, the quantity of dollars is measured on the horizontal axis while the price of dollars (in pounds) is measured on the vertical axis.

The demand curve *DD* slopes down from left to right because the greater the number of pounds that have to be given up for dollars, the fewer will be the quantity of dollars demanded by the British. Another

FIG. 14-1

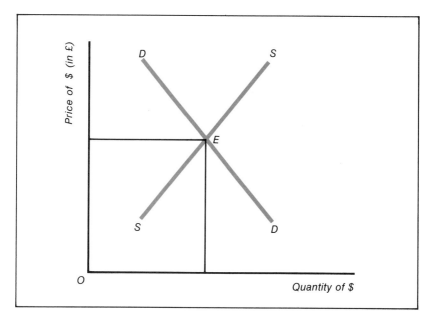

way of expressing the same idea is to say that if Canadian goods become more expensive to the British, the quantity of Canadian goods demanded by the British falls and they would therefore want fewer Canadian dollars. The supply curve *SS* slopes upward from left to right. If the price of dollars falls, Canadians will buy fewer British goods. This means that they will supply fewer dollars to pay for these goods. If the price of dollars rises in terms of British pounds, British goods will become cheaper to Canadians and more will therefore be sold. The Canadians will offer a greater amount of dollars to buy the pounds necessary to pay for the imported British goods.

The intersection of the demand and supply curves determines the exchange rate. If there is an increase in demand for Canadian goods, and hence an increase in demand for Canadian dollars, the value of the Canadian currency will rise. This is referred to as an *appreciation* of the Canadian currency. If the value falls, there is said to be a *depreciation* of the currency.

Many countries now have *fixed* exchange rates, meaning that the value of their currency is fixed in terms of some other currency such as the United States dollar. In order to maintain the currency at its fixed value, the government enters the market and buys or sells foreign exchange. Sometimes it becomes necessary to increase the value of the currency. This is referred to as *revaluation*. If the government reduces the rate at which the currency was fixed, the process is referred to as *devaluation*.

Let us assume that a country on a fixed exchange rate is experiencing an unfavourable balance of trade and that it wishes to improve its situation. This country could devalue its currency. By so doing, its goods will become less expensive to foreigners. At the same time, foreign goods will become relatively more expensive. Thus, by devaluing its currency, a country can stimulate its exports and discourage imports. This will lead to an improvement in its balance of trade and may generate income and employment within the domestic economy.

APPENDIX
QUESTIONS AND ANSWERS

Experience has shown that students in the introductory courses and even some more advanced students do not know how to answer essay-type questions. Quite often they know the material but they just cannot assemble the information in a satisfactory manner when they are asked to do so in a short essay. This appendix is an attempt to teach students how to answer essay questions. The student is exposed to the kind of questions which he is likely to meet in an examination, and provided with examples of the type of answers he is expected to produce.

The student is strongly advised against memorizing any of the answers. Instead, he is expected to study them to see how the facts are put together to answer a particular question. The student may test his ability by attempting to answer the question before reading the answer. He may then compare his answer with the answer provided. If a student does not understand or is not familiar with any of the points made in an answer, he should immediately refer to the text.

Students will usually be asked to answer a certain number of questions in a limited time. Unless the student has mastered the art of answering essay questions, he will find this quite a difficult task. When it comes to mastering essay questions, there is no substitute for practice. The student will find a large number of questions which will equip him with practice material.

Some helpful hints. The following points should prove helpful in answering essay questions.

1. Read the question carefully and be sure you understand what the examiner is asking.
2. When you read a question, a number of ideas will usually come into your head, in a jumbled fashion. Jot down the ideas and then try to arrange them in a manner dictated by the question.
3. Try to express your ideas clearly and to the point.
4. Do not "pad" your answers with irrelevant information. Irrelevant information, no matter how accurate, will earn you no marks.
5. Examples are extremely helpful in illustrating certain ideas. Make use of them.
6. Where possible, use diagrams to illustrate your answers.

QUESTION 1. Do you consider economics to be a science?

ANSWER. To qualify as a science, a discipline must follow a definite procedure. The scientist, in attempting to explain certain phenomena, constructs theories or models. In so doing, he must carefully define words and phrases so as to avoid confusion. He makes certain assumptions which describe the conditions under which the theory is meant to apply. Then he specifies the relationships which exist between the variables under consideration, i.e., he states certain hypotheses. The scientist also proceeds to test his theory to see how well the theory predicts or explains events. The scientist must relate his theory to empirical evidence. This is the scientific procedure. Any discipline which follows this method of enquiry earns the right to be called a science.

In economics, we follow the procedure outlined above, so economics can claim legitimately to be a science. It must be pointed out however, that economics is not an *exact* science like physics, for example. What distinguishes economics and other social sciences from the so-called exact or hard sciences is the difficulty which social scientists face in conducting experiments. The physicist, for example, can enter his laboratory and create the ideal condition for his experiment. The economist, on the other hand, cannot conduct any such controlled experiments. His laboratory is the real world and his subjects of investigation are people. The variables with which the economist works are constantly changing so exact measurement is not possible.

Nevertheless, economists do follow the scientific procedure. They have constructed a large number of models which have proved successful in explaining real world phenomena. There are, for example, models which explain how the price of a commodity is determined in various market situations, and there are models which explain the phenomenon of inflation. The increasing use of mathematical tools in economics has helped economists to be more specific in that the economist is forced to specify clearly and concisely his assumptions and the relationships among the variables with which he is working. The development of econometrics has also helped the economist in testing his theories, and in encouraging the theorist to formulate his theory in a testable manner. It has been demonstrated that economists follow the scientific procedure, thus economics has a legitimate claim to be recognized as a science.

QUESTION 2. (a) Distinguish between microeconomics and macroeconomics. (b) What is the "aggregation problem" in macroeconomics?

ANSWER. (a) The two major branches of modern economic theory are microeconomics and macroeconomics. Microeconomics, also called price theory, is concerned with the behaviour of the individual units that make up the system. Microeconomics deals with the behaviour of consumers, producers and the formation of prices in various types of market structures. It explains the composition of output and the distribution of income among the various factor owners. A British economist, Alfred Marshall, provided the framework for much of modern microeconomics. Because microeconomics is concerned with analysing the behaviour of individual parts of the economy rather than with analysing the problems of the economy as a whole, it is sometimes called partial equilibrium analysis.

Macroeconomics or income and employment theory, as it is sometimes called, deals with the broad aggregates of the system. Macroeconomics studies the behaviour of variables such as total consumption expenditures, total investment, and government spending. It attempts to explain the level of national income and changes in the general level of prices. We owe the development of modern macroeconomics to John Maynard Keynes, another British economist. Macroeconomics is concerned with the operation of the economy as a whole and has therefore earned the name general equilibrium analysis.

It must be pointed out that the distinction made between microeconomics and macroeconomics is largely one of convenience. Certainly, the two branches study different types of problems and use different analytical tools. But a knowledge of each branch is essential for an understanding of the functioning of the economic system.

(b) Since macroeconomics deals with broad economic aggregates, a large number of variables must be added together to obtain a single measure. For example, the macroeconomic concept of total consumption is the sum total of all household consumption, and total business investment is the sum of the investments of all firms. Quite often, the individual units may not be directly conformable to addition. How, for example, do we add the various interest rates to obtain the macro variable called *the* interest rate? This is the problem referred to as the aggregation problem. Some procedure must be devised for aggregating a large number of variables into a single measure. Economists usually overcome the difficulty by using some kind of averaging procedure or by making appropriate assumptions which allow them to perform the aggregation.

QUESTION 3. What is Gross National Product? Discuss some modifications that would have to be made in order to use Gross National Product as a measure of economic progress and human well-being.

ANSWER. Gross National Product (*GNP*) may be defined as the current market value of all goods and services produced by the economy in a year. This measure of total production is often used as a measure of economic progress. An increase in total production means that we have more goods and services to consume and hence a higher standard of living.

In order to use *GNP* as an adequate measure of economic progress, a number of adjustments have to be made. The *GNP* can increase from year to year without any increase in the actual quantities of goods and services produced. This can happen if the prices of goods and services rise. To make meaningful comparisons, and to arrive at an estimate of changes in actual production, we must eliminate the effects of price changes from current *GNP*. This is done by deflating *GNP* by the implicit price deflator. This enables us to express values in constant rather than current dollars. *GNP* in constant dollars, or real *GNP* as it is called, is a better measure than *GNP* in current dollars for purposes of estimating economic progress.

If the real *GNP* of a country increases by ten percent in a year, then obviously more goods and services will be available. But what if the population also increases by ten percent? On an average, people will be no better off. Only if the rate of growth of *GNP* exceeds the rate of growth of the population will people be better off in terms of having more goods and services. The real *GNP* figure must therefore be adjusted by considering changes in the population. By dividing real *GNP* by the total population we obtain a measure called real *GNP* per capita which is a better measure of economic progress. It must be noted however, that *GNP* per capita is only an average which tells us nothing about how total output is distributed among the population.

The *GNP* measures only those goods and services which actually pass through the market. But a number of goods and services actually produced do not get counted in *GNP* because they do not involve any monetary transactions. For example, if a man paints his own house, or does his own landscaping, his services are not counted in *GNP*; and the services rendered by housewives in their own homes are not counted in *GNP*. Although these goods and services do not get counted in *GNP*, they nevertheless increase our standard of living.

Finally, *GNP* measures only the value of goods and services provided by the economy. There are other factors besides goods and services which are indicative of economic well-being. These include leisure, clean and uncrowded cities, unpolluted environments and safe highways—all of which contribute to the quality of life.

QUESTION 4. State the relationship between Gross National Product, Net National Product, national income, personal income, and disposable personal income.

ANSWER. The Gross National Product (*GNP*) is the dollar value of all final goods and services produced annually by the economy. In the process of production, the capital stock suffers a certain amount of wear and tear. This capital consumption or depreciation (D) of the capital stock is subtracted from the GNP to obtain Net National Product (NNP). NNP differs from GNP only by the exclusion of depreciation in the NNP measure.

National income (NI) may be defined as the total income earned by the owners of the factors of production. The entire NNP cannot accrue to factor owners as income because of the existence of indirect business taxes (T_{IB}) which include sales taxes, business property taxes and excise taxes. If indirect business taxes are subtracted from NNP, the resulting figure is referred to as national income (NI). National income may be computed by taking the sum total of employees' compensation (wages, salaries and other labour income), rental income, interest earnings, corporate profits, and income of unincorporated businesses and self-employed persons.

Although the national income is the income earned by the owners of the factors of production, they may not receive what they earn. Personal income (PI) measures the amount of income actually received by households. Before factor owners are rewarded, certain deductions must be made from national income. These deductions include corporate profit taxes (T_c), undistributed corporate profits (P_{un}), and social insurance contributions (SIC). Also, households receive incomes which they do not earn. Such incomes are referred to as transfer payments. Thus if from national income we subtract corporate profit taxes, undistributed corporate profits and social insurance contributions, and then add transfer payments (TR), we will obtain personal income.

Disposable personal income (DI) is the income that people are left with to spend or to save. Personal income is not all available to spend or to save. People have to pay personal income taxes (T_p). When these taxes are subtracted from personal income, the result is termed disposable income.

QUESTION 5. Discuss the economic functions of the government.

ANSWER. The government plays an active role in the economy. In fact, government intervention in the economy has become so intensive that it is now a controversial issue. For purposes of analysis, we can classify government economic activities into four basic functions.

First, the government provides public goods. Public goods have the special quality that once they have been produced, no one can be excluded from them whether or not he paid for their production. This property is referred to as non-exclusion. Perhaps the most popular example of a public good is defence. Once defence is provided, there is no way to prevent some citizens from enjoying the benefits. Some members of the community may argue that a certain type of national defence is unnecessary. They may even be happier if it were not provided, yet they must 'consume' it. Obviously, it would not be profitable for a private business to engage in the production of public goods, because the private enterprise would have trouble selling the goods, not so much because of an absence of demand, but because consumers will consume the goods whether or not they buy them.

The second basic economic function of the government is the regulation of private business. The government often intervenes into the economy by regulating certain prices, controlling the use (or abuse) of natural resources, and protecting the environment.

The third basic economic function of the government is the provision of certain social services considered desirable or essential from the society's point of view. These services include education and health services. If left entirely to private individuals, these services may not be provided in adequate amounts. Many people may prefer to spend their money on other things than, for example, on providing adequate schooling for their children. There may be other people who would be willing to provide such services for themselves, but because of low incomes, they may not be able to do so. The government intervenes and provides such services, paying for them out of taxation. The government also uses its tax power to achieve a more desirable distribution of income in the economy.

Finally, it is now the generally accepted view that the government should assume responsibility for macroeconomic stabilization. Governments have been thrown out of office for what is termed 'mismanagement of the economy.' A government cannot afford to sit idly by and allow high rates of inflation and unemployment to continue. Governments are always busy conducting macroeconomic policy to achieve the objectives of full employment and price stability.

QUESTION 6. Discuss briefly the usefulness of macroeconomic models.

ANSWER. A macroeconomic model is a system of relationships among macroeconomic variables. It is often thought that an economic model is necessarily mathematical, and indeed, most of the sophisticated economic models are mathematical, consisting of a number of equations. This is so because many economic variables lend themselves easily to mathematical expression. But an economic model may take a verbal, a diagrammatical, or a mathematical form. Some types of economic behaviour cannot be easily expressed by means of mathematical equations, and in such cases, a verbal description will have an advantage.

The purpose of a model or theory is to explain some aspect of the economy. By constructing a model, the economist can concentrate on a few "key" variables and observe how changes in these variables affect the system. Without the use of a model, it would be extremely difficult to study the many complex variables that characterize real world situations.

A model is an abstraction from reality, and as such, it has to be modified to make it applicable to the real world. A model of income determination in a closed economy has to be modified to take international trade into consideration, and a simple model which treats the level of investment as a datum has to be modified to be applicable to a situation where the level of investment is dependent upon the rate of interest or on the rate of change of national income.

Macroeconomic models help us to understand complicated economic relationships and thus provide us with a knowledge of how the economy actually works. A good knowledge of the operation of the economy is essential for the formulation of sound economic policies. The insight gained through the use of macroeconomic models can help the practical economist to choose the appropriate policy option when faced with the task of making economic decisions. It is largely through the use of macroeconomic models that governments are able to use fiscal and monetary policies to achieve the macroeconomic objectives of full employment and price stability.

QUESTION 7. Distinguish between national income and national wealth. How are they related?

ANSWER. National income refers to the total earnings of the owners of the productive factors. It may be calculated by adding the amounts paid for the use of land, labour, capital and entrepreneurial services, or by adding the incomes received by the owners of these factors for factor services. National income may also be computed by subtracting capital consumption allowances (depreciation), and indirect business taxes from Gross National Product.

National wealth refers to the nation's stock of buildings, machinery, land, equipment and other economic goods that it has accumulated. An important distinction between national income and national wealth is that one is a flow variable while the other is a stock variable. A flow is the quantity that is forthcoming per period of time, such as a salary of $900 per month or a payment of $40 per week for room and board. Notice that a flow always has a time dimension (per month, per day, etc). A stock on the other hand, is just the quantity existing at a given time, such as $15,000 worth of land at the corner of Sherbrooke and Atwater. A stock does not have a time dimension. Obviously, national income is a flow while national wealth is a stock.

A nation uses its stock of wealth to increase its flow of goods and services, or its income. The greater the national wealth, the greater is likely to be the national income. Also, the greater the national income, the greater is likely to be the nation's ability to add to its stock of wealth.

The distinction between national wealth and national income and also the relation between the two concepts can further be illustrated by considering a nation's manpower. The quantity and quality of the labour stock represents an important part of national wealth. The services provided by the nation's manpower yield a part of national income.

QUESTION 8. What would be the likely economic effects of (a) a reduction in the money supply; (b) an increase in thriftiness?

ANSWER. (a) A reduction in the money supply would tend to raise the rate of interest. This is illustrated in Figure A-1.

FIG. A-1

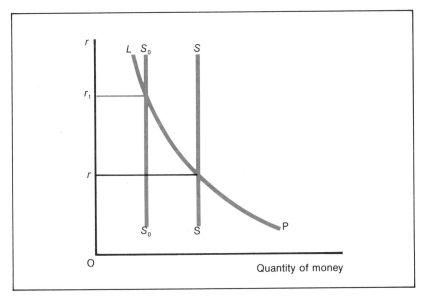

The rate of interest is plotted on the vertical axis while the quantity of money is plotted on the horizontal axis. The curve LP represents the demand for money, and the curve SS represents the money supply which we assume to be given. The rate of interest r is determined by the intersection of LP and SS. A reduction in the money supply from SS to $S_0 S_0$ will cause interest rates to rise from r to r_1 as shown in the diagram.

The increase in the rate of interest is likely to discourage borrowing and may reduce the level of investment. The relationship between the rate of interest and the level of investment is summed up in the marginal efficiency of investment schedule shown in Figure A-2.

FIG. A-2

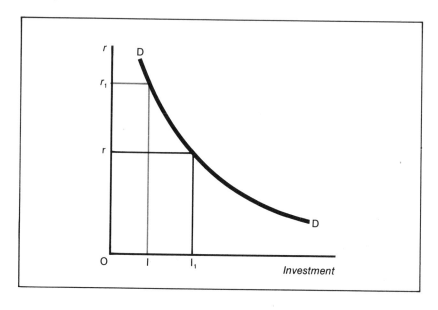

The diagram shows that an increase in the rate of interest from r to r_1 reduces investment from I_1 to I. The increase in the rate of interest may also discourage consumer borrowing and thus reduce consumption spending. Thus we see that a reduction in the money supply, by raising the interest rate, may reduce investment and consumption and hence aggregate demand.

If the economy were in an inflationary situation, the reduction of aggregate demand resulting from the reduction in the money supply would help to reduce the inflation. But if unemployment existed in the economy, then a reduction in the money supply would tend to worsen the unemployment situation.

(b) An increase in thriftiness means that for one reason or another, saving out of a given level of income has increased. This implies, of course, that consumption has decreased. The firms will therefore reduce production causing employment and income to fall. The situation is illustrated in Figure A-3.

Saving and investment are measured along the vertical axis and income along the horizontal axis. We assume that investment (I) is autonomous, so the investment line is horizontal. With a saving line of

FIG. A-3

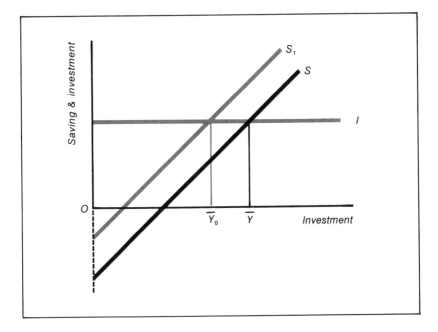

S, the level of income will be $\overline{Y}$. An increase in thriftiness shifts the saving line up from *S* to S_1, and a new level of income, $\overline{Y}_0$, which is less than $\overline{Y}$, is determined. Hence, the effect of an increase in thriftiness is to reduce the level of income in the economy.

QUESTION 9. Why do people save? What determines the amount of saving that will take place in a country?

ANSWER. Saving may be defined as the difference between income and consumption expenditures. Thus, given a level of income, a reduction in consumption implies an increase in saving. People save for a variety of reasons, one of which is to provide for the future. The existence of old-age pensions and other provisions which are made by the government to safeguard people after retirement have caused people to be less concerned with saving for this reason.

A second reason why people save is to be able to make some expenditure in the future. A family may save this year to be able to enjoy a European vacation next year, or a young couple may save with the aim of buying a house in the future. The existence of credit and easy term payment plans will reduce the amount of saving for this purpose. For example, if the downpayment on an automobile is 50 percent, a family would have to save $2,500 in order to purchase a $5,000 automobile. If the downpayment were only ten percent, the family would need to save only $500 in order to purchase the automobile.

People also save in order to leave some form of wealth to their heirs, or they may save and accumulate wealth simply because of the prestige that the acquisition of wealth may bestow on them in their community. Finally, people may save with no particular aim in view, but just out of habit.

The reasons for saving which have been mentioned above will have some effect on the amount of saving that actually takes place. In addition, people's ability to save will be an important determinant of the volume of saving. The most important factor determining the amount of saving is the level of income. Other things being equal, the higher the level of income, the greater the amount of saving that households will be able to undertake.

The rate of interest may also exert some influence on the volume of saving. The prospects of high interest rates on savings may induce households to increase their saving. The existence of institutions such as banks, saving societies and credit unions which facilitate saving will also have some positive effects on the volume of saving that takes place in a country.

QUESTION 10. Differentiate between gross investment and net investment. How are these concepts related to Gross National Product?

ANSWER. Gross investment is total expenditure on capital goods. A portion of this expenditure is used to keep the capital stock intact. During the production period, a certain part of the capital stock is used up and needs to be replaced. This type of investment which simply maintains the capital stock at its existing level is called replacement investment or depreciation. The part of gross investment which actually increases the capital stock is called net investment. Thus gross investment is the sum of net investment and replacement investment.

In calculating Gross National Product—the value of all goods and services produced by the economy—we can add total expenditures by all the spending units. Thus Gross National Product is the sum of consumption (C), investment (I), government spending (G), and net exports ($X - M$). That is,

$$GNP = C + I + G + (X - M)$$

The investment variable in the above equation is gross investment. If replacement investment is subtracted from the Gross National Product, the resulting figure is Net National Product. Moreover, if net investment is undertaken, we will be building up our stock of machines, buildings, equipment, etc., and so increase our capacity to produce a greater output of goods and services. On the other hand, if expenditure on capital is less than what is required to maintain the capital stock at its existing level, then we say we are disinvesting. In this case, we are actually reducing our capacity to produce goods and services. Thus we see that there is a close relation between gross investment, net investment, and Gross National Product.

QUESTION 11. Explain how fiscal policy may be used to reduce unemployment. What difficulties are associated with the use of fiscal policy?

ANSWER. Fiscal policy refers to the government's spending and tax policies aimed at affecting changes in national income and employment. Since the budget is the instrument of fiscal policy, the term 'budgetary policy' is sometimes used. Unemployment may be caused by a deficiency of aggregate demand. The situation is illustrated in Figure A-4.

The economy has settled down at an equilibrium level of income, $\overline{Y}$, which is less than the full-employment level, Y_f. Aggregate demand at full employment is $Y_f A$, but total production is $Y_f B$. In order to achieve full employment, aggregate demand will have to increase as shown by AD_1. This increase in aggregate demand can be promoted by increasing government spending or by reducing taxes. If the government increases its spending, income will rise. As income increases, consumption and probably investment will increase. Thus aggregate demand and employment will increase. If the government reduces taxes, disposable income will increase. This increase in disposable

FIG. A-4

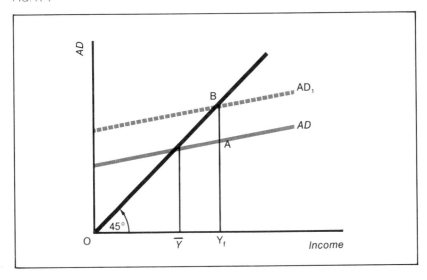

income will generate additional consumption, and probably stimulate investment, causing an increase in aggregate demand and employment.

However, the situation is unlikely to be so easy in the real world. There are two main difficulties associated with fiscal policy. First, it is often difficult to obtain precise estimates of the magnitude of expenditure that would be required to eliminate the unemployment. Because of the pressing need to counteract a situation of unemployment, there is a tendency to apply an overdose of medicine. The deficit may be so large that after the multiplier has had its effect, the economy plunges into a situation of excess demand inflation.

The second difficulty associated with the use of fiscal policy is the time lag. The time that it takes for the effects of fiscal policy to be felt in the economy is very uncertain. It could very well turn out that by the time fiscal policy takes effect, other factors may have caused certain changes in the economic situation so that the effects of fiscal policy may do more harm than good.

QUESTION 12. What measures can a government take to encourage private investment?

ANSWER. A government can take a number of steps to encourage private investment. It must be pointed out that for any particular situation, any of the following suggestions may be undesirable. First, a government may offer special financial assistance to new firms. The assistance may take the form of a loan, or a grant, or some form of subsidy. For example, a provision may be made whereby firms are permitted to deduct a certain percentage of the cost of new capital equipment for tax purposes, or a certain part of the cost of establishing a business may be refunded as soon as the business is established.

Secondly, a government may encourage investment in the private sector by reducing its taxes on business profits. The primary objective of a firm is to earn profits. If a huge portion of these profits is likely to be taxed away, then investment will most likely be discouraged.

A third measure that a government may take to foster private investment is to maintain low interest rates. Low interest rates imply a low cost of borrowing funds, hence low interest rates tend to encourage borrowing and stimulate investment.

A good portion of investment in the private sector is financed, not by borrowed funds, but by undistributed profits. A fourth step a government may take to encourage private investment is to impose a higher rate of taxation on distributed profits than on undistributed profits. There will be an incentive for profits to be re-invested in the businesses rather than given out to shareholders.

Finally, the government can create a climate which is conducive to investment. A favourable investment climate includes the reduction of uncertainties, the promotion of optimistic expectations, and political stability. All these measures are likely to have favourable effects on the level of investment in the private sector.

QUESTION 13. Arrange the following items as they may appear on a commercial bank's balance sheet. Briefly explain each item.

> Deposits
> Loans
> Capital
> Cash Reserves

ANSWER. A balance sheet indicates the assets and liabilities of an institution. The assets represent anything the institution owns, while the liabilities represent the indebtedness of the institution. The following table illustrates how the items in the question may appear on the balance sheet of a commercial bank.

Assets	Liabilities
Cash reserves	Deposits
Loans	Capital

The term "deposits" refers to funds deposited in accounts at commercial banks. These may be demand deposits or notice deposits. Since deposits in a bank account represent amounts that the bank owes its depositors, these deposits are listed as liabilities on the bank's balance sheet. These deposits are of vital importance to a bank because they enable it to make loans and profitable investments from which it derives most of its earnings.

Commercial banks extend loans to households and firms. The difference between the interest the banks charge on loans and the interest which they pay to their depositors is a part of the banks' earnings. A loan is obviously an asset to the bank since the borrower has to repay the loan plus interest charges.

The establishment of a commercial bank requires a huge amount of capital. The bank raises this capital by issuing shares. The capital contributed by the shareholders represents a liability to the bank since it represents the bank's indebtedness to its shareholders.

Commercial banks keep a certain amount of money as cash reserves. This is necessary so that they can accommodate their customers who wish to withdraw funds from their accounts. The cash reserves are held as deposits at the central bank and in the form of notes.

Banks are bound, by law, to keep some reserves. These are called legal reserve requirement. Any reserves held in excess of this legal minimum requirement are termed excess cash reserves. Cash reserves are a part of the assets of a commercial bank.

QUESTION 14. What is the multiplier effect? On what does the value of the multiplier depend?

ANSWER. Investment expenditures accrue to the recipients of these expenditures as income. Some of this income will be spent. This additional expenditure will become income to those who receive it. They, in turn, will spend a part of it thus creating additional income. The process continues until the effect eventually peters out. This process whereby income is multiplied up is called the multiplier effect, and the ratio of the change in income to the change in investment which generates it is called the multiplier.

The value of the multiplier depends on how much of their extra income people will devote to consumption. This is referred to as the marginal propensity to consume. Obviously, the greater the marginal propensity to consume, the greater will be the multiplier effect. In fact, if we assume a closed economy, the value of the multiplier can be calculated by using the formula

$$k = \frac{1}{1 - MPC}$$

where k is the multiplier and MPC is the marginal propensity to consume. Thus given an MPC of 0.8, the value of the multiplier will be

$$\frac{1}{1 - 0.8} = \frac{1}{1 - \frac{4}{5}} = \frac{1}{\frac{1}{5}} = 5$$

Now, if the MPC were 0.6, the multiplier would be

$$\frac{1}{1 - 0.6} = \frac{1}{1 - \frac{3}{5}} = \frac{1}{\frac{2}{5}} = \frac{5}{2} = 2\frac{1}{2}$$

Of course, we could have expressed the multiplier in terms of the marginal propensity to save (MPS). Since $MPC + MPS = 1$, then the multiplier, k, given as $\dfrac{1}{1 - MPC}$, could have been expressed as $\dfrac{1}{MPS}$

The *MPC* is not the only factor which affects the value of the multiplier. Let us suppose that a certain portion of income is used for purchasing imports. The expenditure on imports generates income abroad rather than in the domestic economy. Thus the fraction of extra income that is devoted to imports (i.e., the marginal propensity to import) is another factor which will determine the value of the multiplier. For example, if the *MPS* is 0.25 and there is no foreign trade, then the multiplier will be 4. Let us now admit imports into the analysis. If we assume that the marginal propensity to import is 0.2, then the multiplier will become

$$\frac{1}{0.25 + 0.2} = \frac{1}{\frac{1}{4} + \frac{1}{5}} = \frac{1}{\frac{9}{20}} = \frac{20}{9} = 2\frac{2}{9}$$

It should be noted that although we have concentrated only on the withdrawals, saving and imports, we could have included taxes in the analysis. We can conclude that the value of the multiplier depends on the marginal propensity to withdraw.

QUESTION 15. What is the accelerator principle? What are some of the objections raised with regard to this theory of investment?

ANSWER. An increase in income will cause an increase in demand for consumer goods and services. This increase in demand will give rise to a demand for capital goods to produce the larger volume of consumer goods now being demanded. The capital goods industries will meet this demand for capital goods by increasing their production. This investment induced by the increase in income, will be proportionately larger than the increase in demand for consumer goods and services. This principle is referred to as the acceleration principle. The principle explains why fluctuations in the capital goods industries are more severe than fluctuations in the industries producing consumer goods.

A number of objections have been raised with regard to the acceleration principle. In the first place, it seems to imply that there is no excess capacity in the industries producing consumer goods, so that any increase in demand for consumer goods and services will give rise to an increased demand for equipment used to produce these goods. But in fact, firms are unlikely to purchase new equipment as soon as there is an increase in demand for their products. Instead, they may use any excess capacity which may exist, or they may decide to run existing plant and equipment a little harder, such as going into overtime production.

The accelerator theory also assumes that the supply of capital goods is elastic. The industries producing capital goods may not be able to respond immediately to increases in demand. The implication that there is always excess capacity in the industries producing capital goods is a gross over-simplification of reality.

Finally, it should be noted that an increase in demand is only one possible explanation of investment behaviour. Factors such as the rate of interest, expectations, and the amount of retained earnings are likely to exert some influence on investment decisions.

QUESTION 16. Explain how commercial banks create money. What factors limit the amount of money that banks can create?

ANSWER. Commercial banks create money in the form of bank deposits by making loans which enable them to create deposits. When a customer borrows money from a commercial bank, the bank deposits the amount in an account for the borrower. This deposit is money which the bank has actually created. The bank is required to keep a certain fraction of its deposits as reserves. Any amount over its required reserves can be lent out, thus creating new deposits. Let us illustrate the process with an arithmetic example. Assume that a bank gets a new deposit of $1,000, and that its legal reserve requirement is ten percent. The bank keeps $100 as reserves and makes a loan of $900 to a customer. The bank deposits the $900 in a chequing account for the customer. This new deposit enables the bank to make an additional loan of $810 after keeping $90 as required reserves. A new deposit of $810 is thus created. So far, the bank has created $(900 + 810) = $1,710. The process can continue until the bank's excess reserves have been exhausted.

The banks' ability to create money depends on the amount of money that people deposit in bank accounts. The greater the amount deposited, the greater will be the banks' ability to extend loans and thus create money. The public's desire to hold cash will affect the amount of money deposited in bank accounts. If the public decides to hold a larger amount of money in the form of cash, then the ability of the banks to create money will be reduced.

Another factor which limits the amount of money banks can create is the demand for loans. If customers do not borrow, the banks cannot lend; and if no loans are made, no money creation can take place.

The amount of money that banks can create depends finally on the amount they are required to keep as reserves. The larger the required reserves, the less will be available for loans and thus the less will be the amount of money created.

QUESTION 17. What are the chief functions performed by money? Explain the effects of inflation on any *one* of these functions.

ANSWER. Money performs three main functions. It serves as a medium of exchange, as a store of value, and as a unit of account. When we use money to carry on day to day transactions such as paying for meals in the cafeteria, or buying tickets for public transportation, or buying a textbook at the college bookstore, it is functioning as a medium of exchange. In a modern economy, it is extremely important to have something perform this function. Before the invention of money, exchange was made by means of barter, whereby one good was exchanged directly for another good. This was a very cumbersome and inefficient system, requiring a double coincidence of wants. Money, as a medium of exchange, eliminated the awkwardness of barter.

Individuals may store up money now to be able to buy goods and services in the future. It may be possible to store some commodities, but others are difficult to store because of prohibitive storage costs, or because they are bulky, or because their value diminishes rapidly. Money is a convenient form in which to store up purchasing power.

Money enables us to express values of different commodities in a common unit. The price of a car can be easily compared with the price of a winter vacation if their values are expressed in terms of money. If, for example, the price of the car is $5,000 and the price of the winter vacation is $4,000, we have no difficulty in determining that the car is more expensive than the vacation. Without money performing this function of a unit of account, it would not be so easy to compare the car with the vacation.

During an inflation, money loses its value. A given sum of money will be able to buy a smaller quantity of goods and services. An individual who has saved up a large amount of money may be disappointed at finding that his money is actually worth much less when he is ready to spend it. Realization of this fact causes people to rely less on money as a store of value during an inflation. Any item which is losing its value will not perform the store of value function very well. This explains why, in an inflation, people use real assets such as real estate, rather than money to perform the store of value function.

QUESTION 18. What instruments are available to a central bank for controlling the money supply and credit?

ANSWER. The instruments available to a central bank fall into two categories—general controls and selective controls. There are four instruments under general controls. These are open market operations, the bank rate, the legal reserve requirement, and moral suasion. The central bank can increase the money supply by purchasing securities on the open market. The sellers of these bonds will deposit their cheques in their accounts at commercial banks. These new deposits enable the commercial banks to extend loans and thus increase the money supply. A sale of securities by the central bank on the open market will similarly reduce the money supply.

By increasing the bank rate, the central bank will cause a contraction in credit. Other rates of interest will follow suit and borrowing will be discouraged. A reduction in the bank rate will have an expansionary effect on money and credit.

The central bank can also increase the money supply by lowering the reserve requirements on commercial banks. This will leave the commercial banks with more money to advance loans and thus increase the money supply. A reduction in the money supply can be achieved by raising commercial banks' reserve requirements. The Bank of Canada no longer varies the reserve ratio of commercial banks. However, it has the power to impose a minimum secondary reserve requirement as a control device.

Moral suasion, or jawboning as it is sometimes called, is another tool which a central bank may use to control the money supply. The central bank enlists the cooperation of the commercial banks in carrying out its monetary policy. The small number of commercial banks in Canada makes moral suasion a relatively easy tool to use.

The general controls which we have mentioned affect the overall money supply. Selective controls, on the other hand, regulate credit in specific areas of the economy. A central bank may use these selective controls to restrict credit in order to reduce inflationary pressures. Among the controls which fall within this category are real estate credit controls and consumer credit controls. The central bank may set minimum downpayment requirements for the purchase of consumer goods. Obviously, the higher the minimum required downpayment, the less will be the demand for consumer goods. The central bank may also regulate consumer credit by setting a limit on the time required to pay the balance remaining after the downpayment. A central bank may impose similar controls on real estate credit. The general and selective controls available to the central bank are powerful weapons of money and credit regulation.

QUESTION 19. "The burden of a large national debt, if not paid off in the present generation, will have to be passed on to future generations." Comment *briefly* on this statement.

ANSWER. This statement is just one of the many misconceptions held about the national debt. A nation incurs a debt when its government borrows from the public. The borrowing is done by selling bonds. When individuals and firms buy bonds, they sacrifice goods and services which they could have bought instead. The real cost or burden of the debt must be measured in terms of these sacrificed goods and services. It follows that those individuals and firms who gave up the purchase of fur coats, swimming pools, plant, equipment, larger office space, sports cars, summer vacations, and piano lessons for their children in order to buy bonds are the ones who actually bear the burden of the debt.

If the debt is postponed, its repayment in the future will entail no sacrifice in terms of foregone goods and services. Evidently, there will be some distributional effects following the repayment of the debt. Those who pay the taxes to provide funds to pay off the debt will not generally be the same as those to whom the debt is owed. But in terms of the whole economy, there will be no loss of purchasing power. The losses suffered by those who pay the taxes are exactly offset by the gains accruing to those to whom the debt is owed. Total purchasing power in the economy will be unaffected. It is therefore not possible to pass on the burden of the national debt to any future generation.

QUESTION 20. Distinguish between depreciation and devaluation as applied to a country's currency. How can devaluation improve a country's balance of trade?

ANSWER. The terms "depreciation" and "devaluation" are often confused. Although they refer to the same phenomenon, they belong to different regimes. The exchange rate may be defined as the price of one country's currency in terms of another country's currency. A country may leave the rate at which its currency exchanges for the currency of some other country to be determined by the market forces of demand and supply. Such a system is referred to as a freely fluctuating exchange rate system. If, in this system, the value of a country's currency falls in terms of some other country's currency, we say that there is a depreciation in the country's currency.

A country could also decide to set the value of its currency in terms of some other currency. This is termed a fixed exchange rate. If the country sets the value of its currency at a lower level, we refer to that change as a devaluation of the country's currency. Thus the term depreciation refers to a regime of flexible (freely fluctuating) exchange rates whereas devaluation refers to a regime of fixed exchange rates.

A country's balance of trade refers to the difference between its exports and its imports. A favourable balance of trade is said to exist if exports exceed imports. If imports exceed exports, then an unfavourable balance of trade is said to exist. A country's balance of trade will improve if its exports increase at a faster rate than its imports. If a country devalues its currency, its goods will become relatively cheap to foreigners. This means also that foreign goods will be more expensive. Thus imports will be discouraged and exports encouraged as a result of devaluation, and the country's balance of trade will improve. Our analysis assumes that other countries who buy the products of the country which devalued its currency will not retaliate by devaluing also. If retaliation takes place, then a country cannot hope to improve its balance of trade by devaluing its currency.

ADDITIONAL QUESTIONS

21. Carefully define the Gross National Product of a country. What problems are involved in measuring Gross National Product?

22. "The economy is in equilibrium when saving is equal to investment. Saving is always equal to investment, therefore, the economy is always in equilibrium." Comment on this statement.

23. Define (a) the multiplier, (b) the marginal propensity to consume. Is there any relationship between these two concepts?

24. Explain the Permanent Income hypothesis.

25. Explain the Accelerator Theory of investment. Compare this theory with any other theory of investment with which you are familiar.

26. Explain each of the following terms:
(a) discretionary fiscal policy
(b) automatic stabilizers
(c) fiscal drag
(d) the paradox of thrift.

27. (a) State the Quantity Theory of money.
(b) "An increase in the money supply may have a greater influence on the price level than on economic activity, depending on the circumstances." Discuss.

28. Do you think that a major depression similar to the 1929-33 depression will occur in Canada? Give reasons for your answer.

29. Explain how an increase in the money supply will affect the rate of interest in the Classical Loanable Funds theory.

30. What do you consider to be the most serious *economic* problem facing Canada today? Give reasons for your choice.

31. (a) What functions does money perform in a modern economy?
(b) Should Chargex or Master Charge credit cards be considered as money?

32. "Commercial banks can only lend out money deposited with them, but they cannot increase the money supply." Comment.
33. (a) What is the marginal propensity to consume?
(b) Explain why a redistribution of income from high income earners to low income earners may stimulate an economy.

34. What is an inflationary gap? Explain how fiscal policy may be used to eliminate or reduce an inflationary gap.

35. Many people are concerned about the size of the federal public debt. Do you think there is real cause for alarm?

36. What are the functions of a central bank? Distinguish between general controls and selective controls.

37. "Inflation hurts some people and benefits others, but unemployment hurts everybody." Discuss the above statement.

38. Explain each of the following terms:
(a) balance of payments
(b) exchange rate
(c) devaluation
(d) balance of trade

39. What steps can a country take to improve its balance of trade situation?

40. Do you think that the government should always aim at a balanced budget? Give reasons for your answer.

GLOSSARY

acceleration principle: the relation between a change in income and investment. An increase in income causes an increase in demand for consumer goods which induces an increase in investment which is proportionately greater than the increase in demand.

accelerator theory of investment: the theory which states that investment depends on the rate of change of income.

aggregate demand: total expenditure by all the spending units.

aggregate supply: the value of total production of goods and services in current dollars.

automatic (built-in) stabilizers: fiscal policy measures that are built into the system. They work automatically to dampen economic fluctuations. They are also referred to as non-discretionary fiscal policy.

autonomous investment: investment which is independent of income.

average propensity to consume (APC): the fraction of income devoted to consumption, i.e., the ratio of consumption to income.

average propensity to save (APS): the fraction of income allotted to saving, i.e., the ratio of saving to income.

balance of payments: a record of all international transactions.

balance of trade: the difference between the value of a country's exports and its imports.

balanced budget: a situation where government spending is equal to tax receipts.

balanced budget increase in spending: an increase in government spending which is matched by an increase in taxes.

balanced budget theorem: an increase in government spending accompanied by an equivalent increase in taxes will cause income to increase by the amount of government expenditure.

balance sheet: a statement showing an institution's assets and liabilities.

bank rate: the rate of interest which the central bank charges on loans to the commercial banks. This rate is known as the discount rate in the United States.

barter: trading without the use of money. One good is exchanged directly for another.

budget deficit: a situation in which government spending exceeds its tax receipts.

budget surplus: a situation in which government spending falls short of its tax receipts.

business cycle: relatively regular pattern of ups and downs in economic activity.

capital: a man-made factor of production such as plant and equipment.

capital consumption: the wear and tear of capital stock. This is also referred to as depreciation.

capital-output ratio: the ratio of the total value of the capital stock to the value of total output.

capital stock: the quantity of capital existing at a particular point in time.

central bank: a bank charged with the responsibility of conducting the monetary policy of a country.

closed economy: an economy which does not trade with other economies.

commercial bank: a financial institution which performs a number of important functions including the establishment of chequing and savings accounts. Commercial banks are also known as chartered banks.

consumption expenditures: spending on consumer goods and services.

consumption function: the relationship between consumption and the determinants of consumption.

cost-push inflation: inflation resulting from increases in factor costs.

deflationary gap: the amount by which full-employment output exceeds aggregate demand.

demand: the various quantities that will be purchased at various possible prices.

demand curve: a graph showing the inverse relationship between price and quantity.

demand deposits: deposits in commercial banks which are transferable by cheques.

demand-pull inflation: inflation resulting from an excess of aggregate demand over full-employment output. This is also called excess demand inflation.

depreciation (in national income accounting): see capital consumption.

depreciation (of a country's currency): a fall in the value of a country's currency in terms of the currency of some other country, if the currency of the country in question is left to be determined on the free market by demand and supply.

discretionary fiscal policy: deliberate changes in government spending and taxes designed to promote full employment and price stability.

disposable income: the income available to consumers to spend or to save after income taxes have been paid.

equilibrium: a situation in which there is no tendency for any change to take place.

excess demand inflation: see demand-pull inflation.

excess reserves: reserves held over and above the minimum reserve requirement.

exchange rate: the rate at which one country's currency exchanges for the currency of another country.

factors of production: anything used by the firms to produce goods and services. They are usually classified into land, labour, capital, and entrepreneurial services.

fiat money: money that is not backed by any precious metal.

fixed exchange rate: a system in which the price of a country's currency is fixed in terms of some other currency.

fluctuating exchange rate: a system in which the price of a country's currency is left to be determined by demand and supply.

frictional unemployment: unemployment which results from people changing jobs or from people just entering the labour force.

gold standard: a system in which a country's currency is convertible into gold.

gross investment: total investment consisting of net investment and replacement investment.

gross national product (GNP): the value of all goods and services produced by the economy in a year.

household: the decision-making unit concerned with the purchase of goods and services, and attempting to maximize satisfaction.

hyper-inflation: the most severe form of inflation. The price level increases at an exceedingly fast rate.

indirect business taxes: all taxes imposed on business except corporate profit taxes. They include sales taxes, excise taxes, and property taxes.

induced investment: investment induced by an increase in income.

inflation: a persistent rise in the price level.

inflationary gap: the amount by which aggregate demand exceeds full-employment output.

interest rate: the rate which a debtor pays on a loan from a creditor.

intermediate product: an output of one firm which is used as an input by another firm.

investment: production of capital goods or expenditure on capital goods.

labour force: the number of people employed plus the number involuntarily unemployed.

legal tender: money that must be accepted as payment of a debt, or the debt is considered to be legally discharged.

liquidity preference: the desire to hold assets in the form of money rather than in some other form.

liquidity preference schedule: the relationship between the rate of interest and the quantity of money that people are willing to hold.

liquidity trap: a situation in which increases in the money supply have no effect on the rate of interest.

macroeconomics: the study of broad economic aggregates such as national income, employment and the price level.

marginal efficiency of investment (MEI) schedule: the relationship between the rate of interest and the level of investment.

marginal propensity to consume (MPC): the fraction of extra income that will be spent on consumer goods and services.

marginal propensity to save (MPS): the fraction of extra income that will be saved.

monetary policy: action taken by the central bank to change the money supply and the interest rate in order to achieve full employment and price stability.

monetary theory: a study of the effect of the money supply on income, employment, and the price level.

multiplier: the relation between the change in income and the change in spending which generates the change in income. The multiplier is the inverse of the marginal propensity to save.

national debt: the amount the government owes its creditors. This is also called the public debt.

national income: the total income earned by the owners of the factors of production.

near-money: assets which can easily be converted into the medium of exchange without any appreciable loss of value.

net exports: the value of exports minus the value of imports.

net investment: addition to the capital stock. The difference between gross investment and replacement investment.

net national product (NNP): gross national product minus depreciation.

notice deposit: a deposit at a commercial bank which earns interest and which requires notice before withdrawal.

official reserves: reserves held by a central bank to make international payments.

open market operations: the purchase or sale of government securities by the central bank on the open market.

opportunity cost: any good or service that must be sacrificed in order to obtain a particular good or service.

paradox of thrift: the fact that an increase in saving, other things being equal, reduces income. An attempt to increase saving may result in a reduction in actual aggregate saving.

permanent income hypothesis: the hypothesis that consumption depends on average lifetime income, and not so much on current income.

personal income: total income received by households from all sources.

Phillips curve: the curve showing the trade-off between inflation and unemployment.

precautionary demand for money: the desire to hold money for unexpected contingencies.

price index: a measure of the degree to which prices have changed from one year to the next.

production-possibility curve: a graph showing the various combinations of two goods that an economy can produce with full employment of resources.

public debt: see national debt.

quantity theory (of money): statement that changes in the quantity of money produce proportional changes in the price level.

real GNP: GNP deflated by the price index.

recession: a phase of the business cycle characterized by a general downswing in economic activity. Income and employment tend to fall.

recovery: a phase of the business cycle characterized by a general up-swing in economic activity.

required reserves: the amount the commercial banks are legally obliged to keep in cash or as deposits at the central bank.

saving: disposable income minus consumption.

speculative demand for money: the desire to hold money in anticipation of a fall in asset prices.

stagflation: the simultaneous occurrence of inflation and unemployment.

structural unemployment: unemployment which results from changes in the structure of the economy.

transactions demand for money: the desire to hold money balances for transaction purposes.

transfer payment: a payment made which is not for goods or services produced.

undistributed profits: profits made by a business and not distributed to its shareholders.

velocity of circulation: the average number of times a dollar changes hands.